BUTTERCREAM EXCLUSIVE
CAKE DECORATING

Icing on Top

STEP BY STEP PICTURE
TUTORIALS & RECIPES

Becky Beverly

AUTHOR, PHOTOGRAPHER: BECKY BEVERLY
GRAPHIC DESIGNER: ABIGAIL WALKER
COPY EDITOR: RUTH SCHWALBE

BECKY'S CAKES

TABLE OF CONTENTS

Hello!

Nice to meet you! My name is Becky Beverly. I'm the owner and founder of Icing On Top - Becky's Cakes. I decorate and sell cakes and sugar art from my home, while also offering cake decorating classes in my home and on my YouTube channel! I've named my business as such because I specialize in buttercream and love to add the "something extra" that just brings it all together!

I realize that many of you just know me from my posts on my Facebook page *Icing On Top – Becky's Cakes* or my YouTube channel that goes by the same name. Maybe you just picked up this book because you love buttercream decorating and want more ideas, or you want to learn about buttercream cake decorating.

I think that to know an artist and understand their work, you need to understand who they are and where they come from.

My parents are American, but I was born and raised in India. I now live in Ohio with my hubby and four active kiddos. I decorated my first cake when I was nine, and before you ask- yes- I've definitely posted that picture before on my Facebook business page! My mom and my grandma made our birthday cakes growing up. My mom has always been a tremendous encouragement and let me try decorating cakes when I was little. When I had children of my own, I continued this tradition.

I found that I loved the challenge of trying different techniques and difficult cakes. I was like a sponge absorbing everything I could in online cake classes, YouTube tutorials, books, magazines, and online cake decorating groups! And then came the day that I thought maybe I should start a business selling cakes. As I was toying with the idea, my friend Abigail, believed in me and told me to take the plunge. And so Icing On Top - Becky's Cakes was born!

Since then, I started selling cakes, teaching cake decorating classes in my home, and started my YouTube channel where I share my recipes, cake decorating tips, and sugar art tutorials. I add new video tutorials weekly to my channel!

Every cake decorator has a favorite medium that they like to work with. Mine is buttercream. I love working with it, developing new flavors, and of course eating it! And recently, I've been enjoying pulled and blown sugar art and sculptures!

Let me interject a life lesson from your friendly neighborhood cake decorator- find yourself an encouraging friend to lift you up, be a listening ear, and keep you realistic in your endeavors! Someone who encourages you in your dreams and helps you make them a come to fruition. My friend and neighbor Abigail has been that for me in not only my business, but this book. When I told her I had decided to write a book, she not only cheered me on (as I expected she would!) but she also insisted on doing the layout and design for my book. Abigail does graphic design work for the training/education department of Elizabeth Arden/Revlon, and is an amazingly artist and talented individual.

The world definitely would be a more beautiful place with more "Abigails" in it! I've highlighted her here, but so many of you have been overwhelmingly supportive of my dreams to make the world more beautiful and delicious. From the bottom of my heart, thank you!

I'm also thankful for the opportunity to have written cake decorating tutorials for American Cake Decorating Magazine, and for having had my story featured in Cake Master's Magazine!

I'm excited to see what the future holds for Icing On Top - Becky's Cakes. Thanks for being along for the ride!

Tools of the Trade

Practice and natural ability can only get you so far- if you don't have at least some of this basic hardware, you'll find your cake making and decorating a much more frustrating process! Plan to spend a few dollars at the front end of your confectionary journey, and you'll be so much more satisfied with your results.

And don't worry- I like to cut corners and spend thrifty when I can. So I'm not recommending any equipment that I don't truly think you'll be glad to have.

a) Cake boards: These come in all shapes and sizes!

b) Couplers: These handy screw-on pieces keep your piping tips firmly attached to the bag.

c) Piping tips: I'm only sharing a handful of these- the variety is endless!

d) Russian piping tips: They're a little different than regular piping tips- we'll explore their uses as you read on.

e) Piping bags: Fill these with icing, chocolate, or any other viscous product you'd like to pipe. You can use gallon or sandwich plastic bags in a pinch.

f) Cupcake tins: Some people foolishly call these "muffin tins." But you and I both know their prime purpose is to make tiny frosted cakes.

g) Bench scraper: You'll be glad you have this multipurpose tool in your drawer. You can get them in a variety of sizes and flexibilities.

h) Cake tins: These come in every shape and size you can imagine, and then some. Be sure to grease and flour them before adding batter- you'll thank me later!

i) Turntable: I use this all the time for frosting and decorating.

j) Offset scissors: These are handy for getting piped flowers from point A to B.

k) Flower nails: If you do any sort of flower piping in bulk, this tool will be a lifesaver for your muscles and sanity.

l) Rubber spatula: I really hope you already have one of these in your kitchen. If not, please go out and purchase one immediately.

m) Silicone mat: This is a wonderful tool that you'll

use with any number of conceivable projects- the amount of heat it can withstand is astounding.

n) Offset spatula: Your beautifully smoothed icing will be its own reward for dropping a few dollars on this guy.

o) Apple corer: Okay okay, this is for cupcakes. I find this option to be superior to cupcake corers because 1) it's serrated, 2) it's longer, and 3) it's cheaper. You're welcome.

p) Cupcake liners: I guess you could also use them for muffins...

Recipes

I was constantly frustrated by the lack of good, consistent buttercream recipes, so I took it upon myself to concoct some of my own. Taste is my paramount concern, but I also wanted to be able to create something that would be beautifully piped- and in the case of my base flavors- be a good, strong platform for decorating.

From there, I moved on to fillings and candied fruits. Through trial and error (and a lot of very important taste-test research), I came up with a variety of flavor options that I'm so thrilled to share with you. Enjoy!

(MOCK) AMERICAN
BUTTERCREAM

The reason this buttercream is called "mock" is because I use high ratio shortening instead of butter. You can substitute the shortening for unsalted butter (omit the butter flavoring), but it will not have the same texture. It also will not hold up as well in the heat. One of the benefits of using high ratio shortening is that it melts at a higher temperature.

2 cups high ratio shortening

1 cup milk

3 pounds confectioner's sugar (pure cane)

2 tsp salt

2 tsp vanilla

1/2 tsp butter flavoring

1/4 tsp almond extract

Beat the shortening in your mixing bowl with your paddle attachment to get out the lumps. Scrape the sides. Dissolve the salt in the milk before adding it to the bowl (this will avoid spotting). Add the rest of the ingredients and mix on low for 3 minutes. If you double the recipe, and it covers the paddle of your mixer, then mix on low for 10 minutes. (If you whip it too long on a higher speed, it will create air bubbles in your buttercream that are hard to smooth out.)

BUTTERCREAM

Like the American Buttercream, you can substitute the shortening and butter flavoring for butter, if you prefer. Just know it changes the texture and durability of the final product.

1 cup high ratio shortening

1/2 cup milk

1 1/4 pounds (4 cups) confectioner's sugar (pure cane)

1 tsp salt

1 tsp vanilla

1/4 tsp butter flavoring

1/8 tsp almond extract

1 cup cocoa powder

Beat the shortening in your mixing bowl with your paddle attachment to get out the lumps. Scrape the sides. Sift in the cocoa powder. Add the rest of the ingredients and mix on low for 3 minutes.

STRAWBERRY
BUTTERCREAM

1 cup unsalted butter (room temperature)

1/4 cup fresh strawberry puree

1/2 tsp salt

5 cups confectioner's sugar (pure cane)

2 tsp strawberry extract gel food coloring (optional)

In your mixer, first blend your butter and strawberry puree on medium until well mixed. (Don't skip this step because your frosting will separate if you don't blend the strawberry puree well with the butter.) Add salt and strawberry extract and blend. Add confectioner's sugar and mix on medium until well blended.

Tip: For even more strawberry flavor, put some freeze dried strawberries in the blender and blend. Hand mix in 3 tablespoons to your buttercream.

LEMON
BUTTERCREAM

1 cup unsalted butter (room temperature)

1/4 cup fresh lemon juice

1/2 tsp salt

1 1/2 pounds (6 cups) confectioner's sugar (pure cane)

1 heaping TBS lemon zest

In your mixer blend your butter and lemon juice on low until well mixed with your paddle attachment. (Don't skip this step because your frosting will separate if you don't blend the lemon juice well with the butter.)

Add salt and confectioner's sugar and mix on low until well blended, scraping sides.

You can leave it in its natural pale color or add a drop of lemon yellow gel food coloring.

Hand mix in the lemon zest.

For a stiffer frosting, you can add more confectioner's sugar 1/4 cup at a time until it reaches the desired consistency.

BLUEBERRY
BUTTERCREAM

4 cups confectioner's sugar (pure cane)

1 cup unsalted butter (room temperature)

1/4 cup fresh blueberry purée

3 Tbsp. freeze dried blueberries (using blender to make it a powder)

2 tsp blueberry emulsion

1 tsp salt

Blend butter and fresh blueberry purée on medium until fully blended (about 5 minutes). Add the rest of the ingredients and blend on low until fully mixed. For thicker buttercream add an extra cup of confectioner's sugar and blend again on low.

BLACKBERRY
BUTTERCREAM

1 cup unsalted butter (room temperature)

6 oz fresh blackberries

5 cups confectioner's sugar (pure cane)

1/2 tsp salt

2 tsp blackberry extract

3 Tbsp. ground freeze dried blackberries

1 tsp. granulated sugar

In a grinder grind up your freeze dried blackberries and set aside. Blend your 6 oz. of fresh blackberries to make a purée. Use 1/4 cup of the blackberry purée to the buttercream recipe. Use the remainder of the blackberry purée with one tsp. of granulated sugar mixed in for the drizzle.

In your blender with the paddle attachment, mix butter and the 1/4 cup of purée on medium for about 5 minutes. Scrape the sides. Add confectioner's sugar, salt, extract, and freeze dried blackberries. Mix on low until well incorporated.

CHERRY
BUTTERCREAM

1/4 cup cherry purée

1 cup unsalted butter (room temperature)

5 cups confectioner's sugar (pure cane)

1/2 tsp salt

2 tsp cherry extract

Blend cherry purée and butter on medium speed until well blended. Add the rest of the ingredients and mix on low until fully mixed.

KEY LIME
BUTTERCREAM

1 cup unsalted butter (room temperature)

1/4 cup fresh lime juice

1/2 tsp salt

1 1/2 pounds (6 cups) confectioner's sugar (pure cane)

1 heaping Tbsp. lime zest

In your mixer, using your paddle attachment, blend your butter and lime juice on low until well mixed. (Don't skip this step because your frosting will separate if you don't blend the lime juice with the butter).

Add salt and confectioner's sugar and mix on low until well blended, scraping sides. You can leave it in its natural pale color or add a drop of leaf green gel food coloring.

Hand mix in the lime zest.

For a stiffer frosting, you can add more confectioner's sugar 1/4 cup at a time, until it reaches the desired consistency.

MANGO
BUTTERCREAM

4 cups confectioner's sugar (pure cane)

1 cup unsalted butter (room temperature)

1/4 cup fresh mango purée

3 Tbsp. freeze dried mango (using blender to make it a powder)

2 tsp mango extract

1 tsp salt

Blend butter and fresh mango purée on medium until fully blended (about 5 minutes). Add the rest of the ingredients and blend on low until fully mixed. For thicker buttercream add an extra cup of confectioner's sugar and blend again on low.

4 cups confectioner's sugar
(pure cane)

1 cup unsalted butter
(room temperature)

1/4 cup fresh pineapple purée

3 Tbsp. freeze dried pineapple
(using blender to make it a
powder)

2 tsp pineapple extract

1 tsp salt

Blend butter and fresh pineapple
purée on medium until fully
blended (about 5 minutes). Add
the rest of the ingredients and
blend on low until fully mixed.
For thicker buttercream add an
extra cup of confectioner's sugar
and blend again on low.

PINEAPPLE
BUTTERCREAM

PEANUT BUTTER
BUTTERCREAM

1 cup unsalted butter (room temperature)

1 cup peanut butter

5 cups confectioner's sugar

1 tsp vanilla

1/2 tsp salt

1/2 cup milk

Blend peanut butter and butter on low until fully incorporated, scraping the sides of the bowl (about 5 minutes). Add confectioner's sugar, salt, vanilla, and milk and blend on low for 5 to 10 minutes or until fully incorporated. Make sure to scrape the sides.

OREO
BUTTERCREAM

1 cup high ratio shortening

1/2 cup milk

1 1/2 pounds (6 cups) confectioner's sugar (pure cane)

1 tsp salt

1 tsp vanilla

1/4 tsp butter flavoring

1/8 tsp almond extract

1 cup finely crushed Oreo cookies

Beat the shortening first, in your mixing bowl with your paddle attachment, to get out lumps. Scrape the sides. Add the rest of the ingredients and mix on low for 3 minutes. Hand mix in the crushed Oreos. (An easy way to crush the Oreos is to put the Oreos in a large ziploc bag and crush with a rolling pin.)

You can substitute the shortening for unsalted butter (and omit the butter flavoring) but it will not have the same texture. It also will not hold up as well in the heat. One of the benefits of using high ratio shortening is that it melts at a higher temperature.

PUMPKIN
BUTTERCREAM

1 cup unsalted butter
(room temperature)

1/2 cup pumpkin purée

1 tsp salt

1 tsp vanilla

1 1/2 tsp pumpkin spice

1/2 tsp cinnamon

6 cups confectioner's sugar
(pure cane)

(Optional: sprinkle a pinch
of nutmeg on top after
decorating cupcakes or cake)

In your mixer, with the
paddle attachment, blend
butter and pumpkin puree
on low until well blended.
Add the rest of the
ingredients and mix on low
until fully incorporated.

PEPPERMINT
BUTTERCREAM

1 cup high ratio shortening

1/2 cup milk

1 1/2 pounds (5 cups) confectioner's sugar (pure cane)

1 tsp salt

1 tsp vanilla

2 tsp peppermint extract

In your mixer, using your paddle attachment, beat the shortening to get out the lumps. Scrape the sides. Add the rest of the ingredients and mix on low for 3 minutes. *Optional - add a drop of leaf green gel food coloring to have a green peppermint look.

You can substitute the shortening for unsalted butter (and omit the butter flavoring) but it will not have the same texture. It also will not hold up as well in the heat. One of the benefits of using high ratio shortening is that it melts at a higher temperature.

CARAMEL
BUTTERCREAM

1 cup unsalted butter

2 cups brown sugar

1/2 cup milk & 1 Tbsp. milk

5 1/2 cups confectioner's sugar (pure cane)

2 tsp salt

In a large sauce pan on medium low heat, add butter, brown sugar, & 1/2 cup milk. Mix until butter is melted and brown sugar is dissolved. Stop mixing and turn up to medium heat. Once it reaches boiling, let it bubble for five minutes and then remove from heat.

Pour into a separate bowl, cover, and set aside until caramel is COMPLETELY room temperature.

Mix room temperature caramel in mixer with paddle attachment on low for a couple minutes. Add confectioner's sugar and salt. Mix on low for about a couple minutes, scraping the sides. Add milk and mix on low for about five minutes.

CARAMEL
FILLING + DRIZZLE

1 cup unsalted butter

2 cups brown sugar

1/2 cup milk & 1 Tbsp. milk

For the filling and drizzle, repeat the caramel making process using all of the same ingredients except the confectioner's sugar and salt.

In a large sauce pan on medium low heat, add butter, brown sugar, & 1/2 cup milk. Mix until butter is melted and brown sugar is dissolved. Stop mixing and turn up to medium heat. Once it reaches boiling, let it bubble for five minutes and then remove from heat.

MAMA'S FUDGE
FILLING

1 cup butter

3 cups granulated sugar

1 cup cocoa powder

1/2 tsp salt

1 cup milk

Melt butter in sauce pan. Add sugar, salt, milk, and sift in cocoa powder. Cook on medium low stirring constantly for 20 minutes or until smooth and sugar is dissolved.

Cool completely before using as cupcake filling or use as an ice cream topper.

PEANUT BUTTER
FILLING

1/2 cup unsalted butter (room temperature)

1 1/2 cup peanut butter

1 tsp vanilla

2 cups confectioner's sugar (pure cane)

1/2 cup milk

Mix butter and peanut butter on low until fully incorporated, scraping the sides. Add vanilla and confectioner's sugar. Mix on low. Add milk and mix on low until fully incorporated, scraping the sides again.

Fill the middle of your cupcakes or cakes with this. It's paired well with my peanut butter buttercream on top.

BLUEBERRY, RASPBERRY, BLACKBERRY, STRAWBERRY, OR CHERRY FILLING

You can use this same method for making raspberry, blackberry, cherry, or strawberry filling. Just replace the fresh blueberries with the other fresh fruit.

3 pints fresh blueberries

1/3 cup water

1/3 cup sugar

2 Tbsp. lemon juice

3 Tbsp. Corn Starch

Place blueberries, lemon juice, water, and sugar in a large sauce pan and cook on medium heat.

Occasionally stir and crush blueberries and let boil for about 15 minutes. In a separate bowl mix corn starch with equal parts cool water. While the blueberry mixture is boiling on medium heat, add corn starch and whisk fast until fully incorporated (about 5 minutes). Remove from heat.

Make sure filling is completely cool before adding it to cake or cupcakes.

For the strawberry filling, first dice the strawberries before adding them to the sauce pan. For the cherry filling, first pit the fresh cherries before adding them to the sauce pan.

CANDIED
STRAWBERRIES

1/2 cup water

1/2 cup sugar

Strawberries

Place water and sugar in a sauce pan and cook on medium high, stirring occasionally, until it comes to a boil. Set saucepan aside until it cools.

Thinly slice strawberries. The thinner you slice them, the quicker they will dry in the oven. Prepare your cookie sheet by covering it with parchment paper or a silicone baking mat. Dip the thinly sliced strawberries one at a time in your cooled syrup, let it drip, and then place it on your prepared cookie sheet. The next step is to completely dry your strawberries. Turn your oven on a very low setting, 200 degrees F. Then cook for 1-3 hours until the strawberries are dried but not browned or burned. The reason there is such a wide time range is because it all depends on how thinly you have sliced your strawberries. They will be slightly tacky feeling. Once you cool the strawberries completely, you can remove them from your cookie sheet.

CANDIED
LEMONS

3 lemons

1 cup of granulated sugar

1 cup of water

Combine sugar and water in skillet. Squeeze in half a lemon (2 Tbsp. lemon juice) over a strainer. Mix on high until it's boiling, then turn down to medium low.

Thinly slice a couple lemons and lay them in the skillet. Cook on medium low for 20 minutes. Flip the lemons over and cook another 15 minutes.

Place the lemons on a piece of wax paper to cool. It can take 3-4 hours to completely cool and firm up.

They will be a firm gummy texture when they're ready.

Just about anybody can follow directions and make a cake, but most people think a beautifully decorated confection is out of their abilities. The truth is, with a few simple decorating tricks in your personal arsenal of skills, you should be able to create a beautiful masterpiece.

The best part is it will be totally edible! Get ready to feast your eyes... and your belly.

Basic Cake Decorating

BASIC
RELEASE, LEVEL & FROST

Tools you'll need: Here are some basic cake decorating tools that we'll be using: cake level, large serrated knife, quick icer tip, off-set spatula, bench scraper, large pastry bag, and turntable.

RELEASE

To get a cake to cleanly release from a pan with little effort is actually easier than you would think. Just make sure your pan is well prepared before adding your cake batter.

STEP 1

Put a large dab of shortening in your pan and completely grease your pan ensuring that every spot is covered.

STEP 2

Place a handful of flour in the pan and shake it around until the entire pan is covered in flour.

Tip the pan upside down and tap it to get rid of the excess flour. Check your pan to make sure there are no shiny spots and that it has been completely covered. If there are any shiny spots, repeat the steps just for those spots.

*Cake tip: You can also achieve releasing a cake by using "cake goop". You can create your own "cake goop" by adding 1 cup oil, 1 cup shortening, and 1 cup flour, mixing well, and storing it in a well-sealed container. You can then use the cake goop to completely coat your pans instead.

STEP 3

Now you're ready to put your batter in your prepared pan. Fill the cake pan half full and bake according to your recipe. I always check mine before the time limit set because you can always keep your cake in longer, but a dry or burnt cake can't be fixed. I use a toothpick to prick the center of my cakes. If it comes out clean and not wet, then the cake is done and can be removed from the oven. Give your cake a couple minutes in the pan before the next step.

STEP 4

Using a cooling rack, simply flip the cake pan on the rack and it should come out easily. If it's a larger cake, place the rack on top of the cake. Firmly press your hand on the center of the rack which is on top of the cake and with your other hand firmly pressed on the bottom of the cake pan, flip it over so that the rack is on the bottom and your cake pan is on the top. This will help a larger cake not to crack during the flip.

LEVEL

To get a nearly perfect looking cake, especially when stacking layers or torting, leveling is very important. A cake level is adjustable depending on how thick you want your cake layers.

STEP 1

Using the cake level, gently work it through the cake. Sometimes this can be achieved by gently sawing it back and forth through your cake. Usually you will have to get it started using a large serrated knife and using it whenever the cake level doesn't easily pull through the cake. The cake level is basically a thick wire which is why you need the serrated knife at times.

FROST

I frost most of my cakes with my (Mock) American buttercream recipe. It's made with high ratio shortening which holds up well in the heat and has a lovely smooth texture. Almost everyone I know loves the flavor! I use it for both wedding and birthday cakes.

STEP 1

Using the quick icer tip, cut the pastry bag so that the tip will fit half way in the bag without popping out. Then fill the bag with buttercream. Using the tip to apply the buttercream makes it easier to get the icing on where you want it and at the level that you want it quickly. I always start with the top of the cake when using this traditional method.

Now using the off-set spatula, smooth the buttercream on top.

STEP 2

Again, use the quick icer to put buttercream on the sides of our cake. As you apply pressure squeezing the buttercream out of your bag, slowly turn your turn table.

Keep piping around until the top layer is slightly taller that the top of your cake.

STEP 3

Using the bench scraper at a 90 degree angle, with the bottom of the scraper flat on the cake board, scrape it all around the cake.

STEP 4

Next, you'll do the "knock down," using your off-set spatula. Starting on the outside and pulling in towards the center of the cake at a 45 degree angle to the top of the cake, smooth the buttercream and spin the cake to the next section until the whole top is flat and smooth.

*Sometimes one layer of buttercream is enough, but if you spot any part of the cake or crumbs then consider this your crumb coat. Pop it in the fridge for 30 minutes. Then add a second layer of buttercream with the quick icer and scrape it one last time.

STEP 5

Finally, if you want it extra smooth, place the bench scraper and off-set spatula in boiling water. Make sure to wipe your tools with a paper towel each time you smooth the buttercream. Do a small section at a time. Dip your tool back in the boiling water, wipe the tool, and then smooth. The hot tools help smooth out the buttercream.

PRACTICE
PIPING
SHEET

I developed these practice sheets for my classes that I teach at home. I found that it helped to first practice the motion that you'd be doing on the cake on the practice sheets first, gain your confidence, and then pipe it directly on the cake.

When you turn the next few pages, you'll see my practice sheet. You can put wax paper over the book and practice right here or scan the QR code provided to take you directly to a download link and from there you can print it.

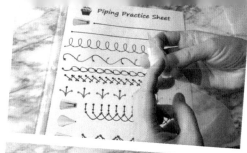
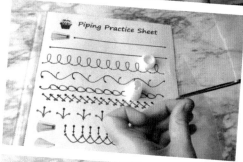
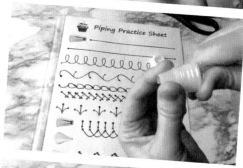
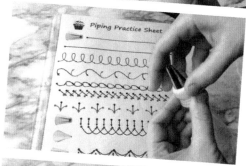
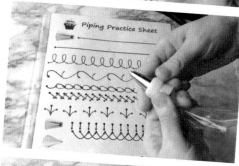
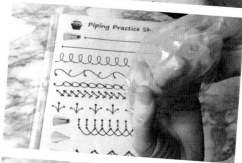

ASSEMBLE THE PIPING BAG

First we need to assemble our piping bag. If you don't have a coupler, you can place the tip directly in the bag following the same procedure we used to put the coupler in. The coupler has two pieces to it, the main body and the plastic ring which holds your tip in place. The main body of the coupler will stay in your piping bag.

STEP 1

You only want the coupler to sit half way out of your bag, anymore and it will pop out when you apply pressure to the buttercream. So check to see where the halfway mark would be before you cut.

STEP 2

Cut the bag. You can always cut more if you need to, but if you cut the bag too much, you won't be able to use it.

STEP 3

Put the coupler in the bag and squeeze it through the hole. It should rest snugly in the bag.

STEP 4

Place your tip on the coupler and secure it in place with the plastic ring. The coupler is especially beneficial when you are going to be using multiple tips with the same color buttercream. You'll easily be able to switch out your tips and only have to use one bag. *Note: larger tips will not fit in a standard coupler.

STEP 5

Fold your bag in half.

STEP 6

You can easily hold your bag now and fill it with buttercream. Once the bag is half full with buttercream (less if you're a beginner and you need more control), pull the bag back up and shake the buttercream down to the tip. Then press it down with your hand and twist the bag so that the buttercream stays tight towards your tip and won't come back up and spill out of your bag. Hold the twist in place with your thumb and first finger. Every time you pipe, you will simply apply pressure with your fingers and the buttercream will come out the tip. As you pipe out your buttercream, you will need to adjust your bag to keep it tight by pressing the buttercream down and twisting again as you go to keep the buttercream tightly down in your bag.

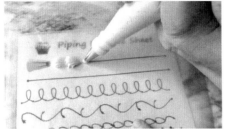

STRAIGHT SHELL BORDER

This is the most common border and is a great one to start practicing on. These different motions will work with different sized open star tips. We'll be working with a medium sized open star tip. The number on the side of this one is a 21, but this will work with anything similar in size. You can create different looks with larger star tips.

STEP 1

Holding our bag at about a 45 degree angle to the surface, apply pressure to the top of the buttercream and this will push the buttercream out through the tip. To create the shell you will apply pressure to the bag, let the buttercream build a shell, release the pressure on the bag, and pull.

STEP 2

Pipe the next shell on the tail of the previous one. You can go around the entire top or border of a cake with this straight shell. Try to keep all the shells uniform by applying the same amount of pressure for the same length of time for each one.

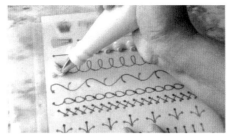
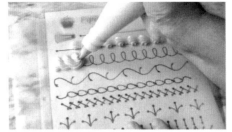

E MOTION

Using the same tip, you can create a thicker border around the top of your cake using the "e" motion. This border also looks great with larger star tips.

You will use continuous pressure with this one, basically piping a cursive e for the entire circumference of your cake.

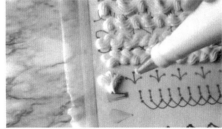

FLEUR DE LIS

This is a French decorative design.

STEP 1

Pipe a shell straight down.

STEP 2

Pipe two shells on either side of the first one. Both of these side shells will come in at an angle towards the middle of the center shell.

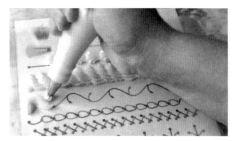

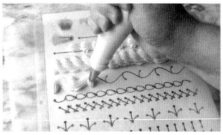

REVERSE SHELL

I like to use this one as a top or bottom border around my cakes.

STEP 1

You're going to pipe a swirl in one direction, release the pressure and end the swirl.

STEP 2

Reverse and pipe the next swirl over the last one's tail.

STEP 3

After you get the motion down, you can also pipe these swirls so that they're shorter and tighter together.

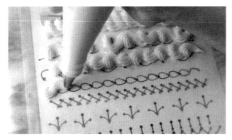

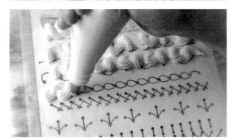

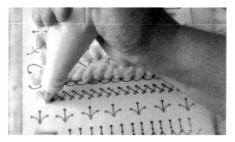
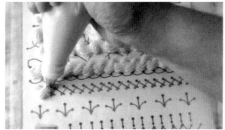

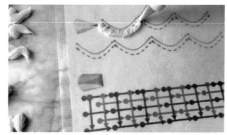
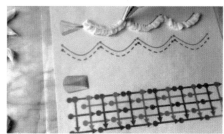

THE ROPE

This maneuver can be used as a border around the top or bottom of your cake. When making flower basket cakes, I especially like the rope to look like it ties together my basket on either the top or on both the top and bottom borders of my cake.

This basically looks like a sideways S.

STEP 1

Pipe your first sideways S using continuous pressure on your S and releasing pressure at the end of your S while you're pulling away.

STEP 2

In the curve of your last S, pipe the next S.

STEP 3

Continue piping S until you reach all around your cake.

THE X

I like to use this motion when creating a knit look like a buttercream scarf.

STEP 1

Apply pressure and make one side ways line, applying pressure through the line, release the pressure at the end, and keep pulling.

STEP 2

Switch directions and pipe over the tail of the last line.

STEP 3

Continue your X motion for the whole line.

BUNTING

We're going to switch out our tip with a small petal tip like a 104. You can use a larger petal tip like a 124 if you want a larger ruffle.

STEP 1

Applying continuous pressure, with the narrow end or the tip facing down, pipe a shallow U, shaking your wrist to create a ruffly look. The dotted line will help you remember to shake your wrist as you go.

STEP 2

Pipe an overlapping U over the top half of the ruffle. This time you won't shake your wrist but rather pipe it straight with the narrow end of your tip still facing down.

DECORATIVE SIDE BORDERS

STEP 1

First pipe shells straight down all around the top side of your cake.

STEP 2

Switch out your tip to a small writing tip like a number 5. This part is a little harder to practice on a flat surface because on the side of the cake we will be using gravity to pipe a string, let gravity drop it down, skip a shell, and secure it to the targeted shell by touching our tip to the bottom of that shell. Continue all the way down your line of shells, making sure to skip one.

STEP 3

Now you will repeat the exact same thing on all the skipped shells.

STEP 4

Finally you will place a small dot on all the meeting points of the shell and rope.

PIPING LEAVES

Use any leaf tip, like a 366 or 352 (they look like a V).

BASKET WEAVE

I love using this on my flower basket cakes! You can use any basket weave tip depending on how large of a basket weave you want. I'm using the tip number 47 for this practice.

STEP 1

First, you will pipe a straight line down using continuous pressure until you reach the bottom.

STEP 2

Starting a little bit before your line, pipe straight across it, overlapping it on both sides. You will leave a gap the size of your tip in between each line.

STEP 3

Pipe straight down again, overlapping the ones you just piped across but leaving a small gap between the last vertical line and this one.

STEP 4

Fill the gaps by piping horizontal lines again, straight across and overlapping your previous vertical line.

STEP 5

Repeat again by piping the next vertical line straight down, covering the tails of the last horizontal lines.

STEP 1

Pipe, applying pressure, let it build.

STEP 2

Release the pressure and pull.

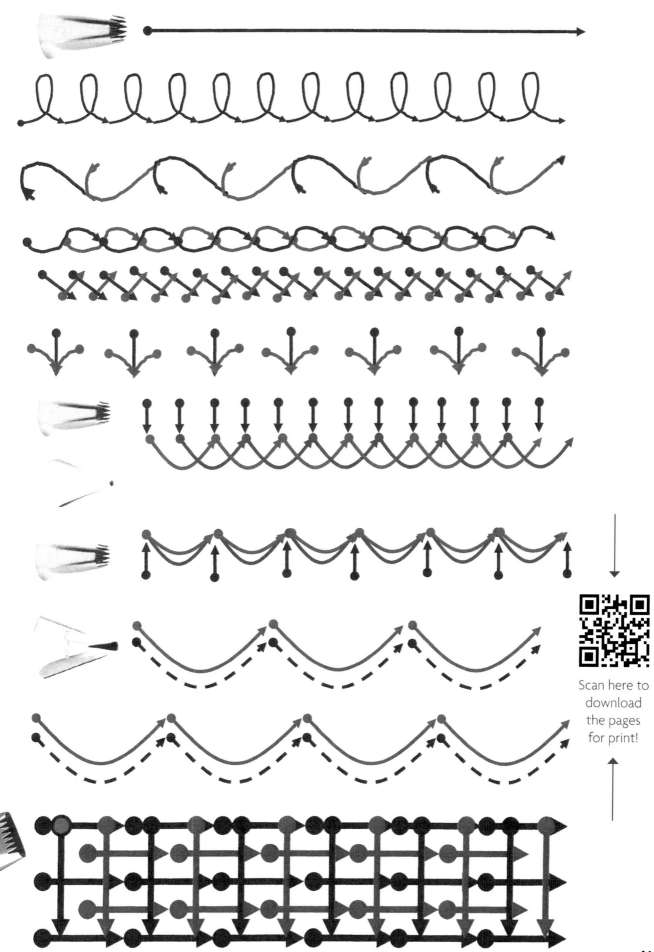

Scan here to
download
the pages
for print!

41

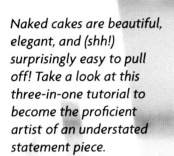

Naked cakes are beautiful, elegant, and (shh!) surprisingly easy to pull off! Take a look at this three-in-one tutorial to become the proficient artist of an understated statement piece.

Tools you'll need:: Quick icer tip, off-set spatula, bench scraper, large pastry bag, turn table, cake boards for each tier, dowel rod (or skewer), smoothie straws (or dowel rods), filling, and buttercream.

STACK, FILL & FROST
A SEMI NAKED CAKE

FILL

STEP 1

Place a little bit of buttercream on your cardboard cake circle to act as your glue and then place your first layer of cake on top. I like to use a large circle of cardboard under the cardboard holding the cake so that I have something to carry the cake on to place in the fridge. Smooth a thin layer of buttercream on the first layer using an offset spatula.

STEP 2

Using a pastry bag, pipe a dam of buttercream around the very edge of your cake in order to keep your filling from leaking.

STEP 3

Spoon or pipe your filling on your cake, making sure not to fill it higher than the dam of buttercream.

STEP 4

Smooth the filling with an off-set spatula.

STEP 5

Place the next leveled cake layer on top.

STEP 6

Use a level to make sure that your buttercream and filling is level. Press down on either side as needed until the bubble rests in the middle of your level indicating that you have a perfectly level cake.

STEP 1

You can use a quick icer tip to quickly and easily apply buttercream to your cake. Apply the buttercream to the top of your cake first.

STEP 2

Scrape it off using your off set spatula.

STEP 3

Use the quick icer tip to apply buttercream around the sides of your cake.

STEP 4

Scrape the excess frosting off using your bench scraper, but not getting so close as to start scraping the cake itself and creating crumbs. Place it in the fridge so that it is chilled before stacking.

FROST

Note: The bottom tier of the cake can be frosted right on the cake drum. The other tiers should be frosted on a cardboard cake circle the same size as the cake tier. A small hole should be cut out in the middle of the cardboard so that the dowel rod can easily be inserted through all the layers. This cake has two layers on each of the three tiers. Each layer is approximately an inch and a half, making each tier over three inches high after adding the filling.

STACK

STEP 1

Place a smoothie straw in your bottom tier and press down until the first straw touches the bottom board.

STEP 2

Mark your smoothie straw right where it touches the top of your buttercream so that when you cut it, it will be flush with the top of your buttercream and not press down and squish your buttercream layer. Pull it out of your cake and cut it.

STEP 3

Mark the rest of the smoothie straws needed for that layer and cut them to the same size of the original one.

STEP 4

Place all of the smoothie straws about a half inch in from where the cake above it will rest. I use about one smoothie straw per inch of cake that it will be supporting. If the cake resting on it is a 6 inch round, I use 6 smoothie straws.

STEP 5

Remove the second tier from the fridge. Carefully slide a bench scraper under the cake board of the cake. Use your cake scraper and your hand to support your cake as you place it on top of your first tier. Make sure that the cake is centered before stacking your next tier.

STEP 6

Follow the same process to stack your next tier.

STEP 7

When all your tiers are stacked, use your wooden skewer to anchor all the tiers together. Make sure you place the skewer in the middle of your top tier and pierce through all the tiers. Each of your tiers are on top of a cardboard cake circle that has a little hole in the middle for this very purpose.

STEP 8

Pipe a thin layer of buttercream around each tier to create a more seamless look between each tier.

45

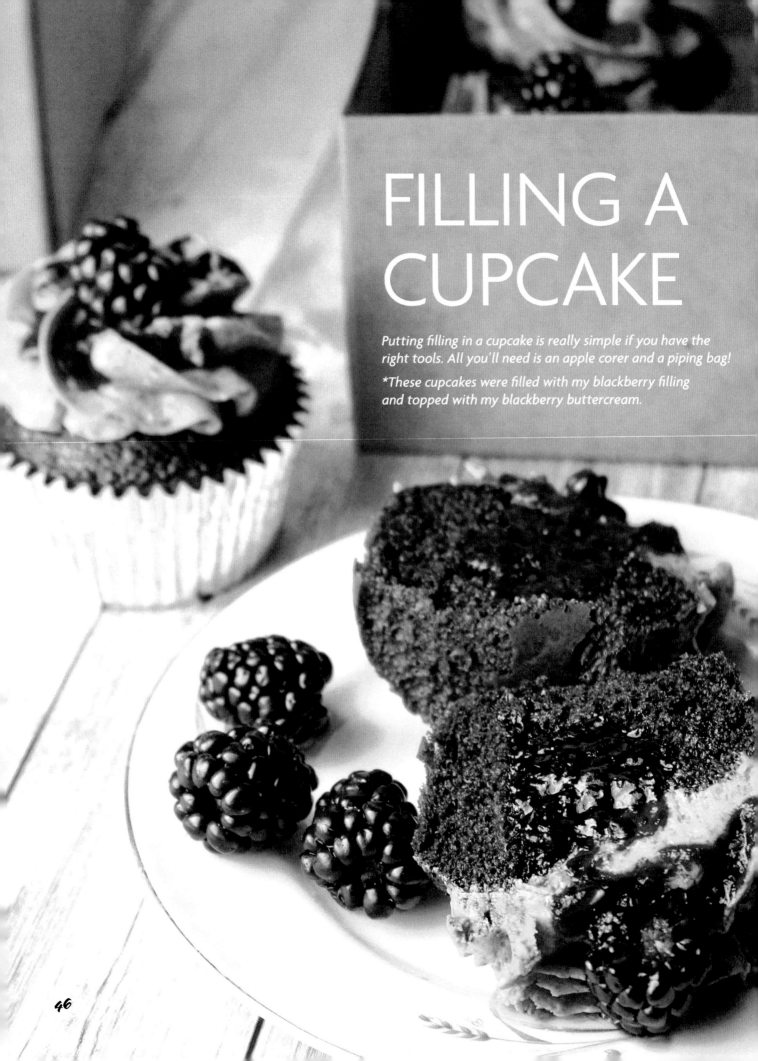

FILLING A CUPCAKE

Putting filling in a cupcake is really simple if you have the right tools. All you'll need is an apple corer and a piping bag!

*These cupcakes were filled with my blackberry filling and topped with my blackberry buttercream.

STEP 1

Using your apple corer, gently press into your cupcake, twisting the corer back and forth as you do. Only go down about 3/4 of the way into your cupcake. You'll want to make sure that there is enough cupcake in the bottom to support your filling.

STEP 2

Pull your corer out and open it like a clothes pin to release the piece of cupcake. (Some people choose to trim it and keep the tops to later replace after filling, but I prefer to fill my cupcakes as much as possible so I don't bother keeping the tops.)

STEP 3

After doing about 3 cupcakes, you'll find that a lot of cupcake is sticking to your apple corer. I like to wipe it off with a paper towel after every three cupcakes to keep it working effectively.

STEP 4

Prepare your piping bag with filling. I like to fold it in half, using a cup to hold it upright. Next you can scoop or pour the filling right into the bag while the cup holds your bag.

STEP 5

Snip off the end of your bag and squeeze the bag into each hole.

STEP 6

Pipe your buttercream directly over the hole and around it in a rosette. This is the same way we did it when decorating our easy, fancy cupcakes.

SPRINKLE SURPRISE CUPCAKES

STEP 1

For these fun cupcakes with a sprinkle surprise inside, spoon in sprinkles instead of filling!

Next, pipe your buttercream right over the top center, as if you're piping a rosette. (I used a 1M tip for these.)

STEP 2

Using continuous pressure, pipe around the center.

STEP 3

Continue piping around, making a smaller swirl on top of the last one.

STEP 4

Once you return to the center, release the piping pressure and pull up.

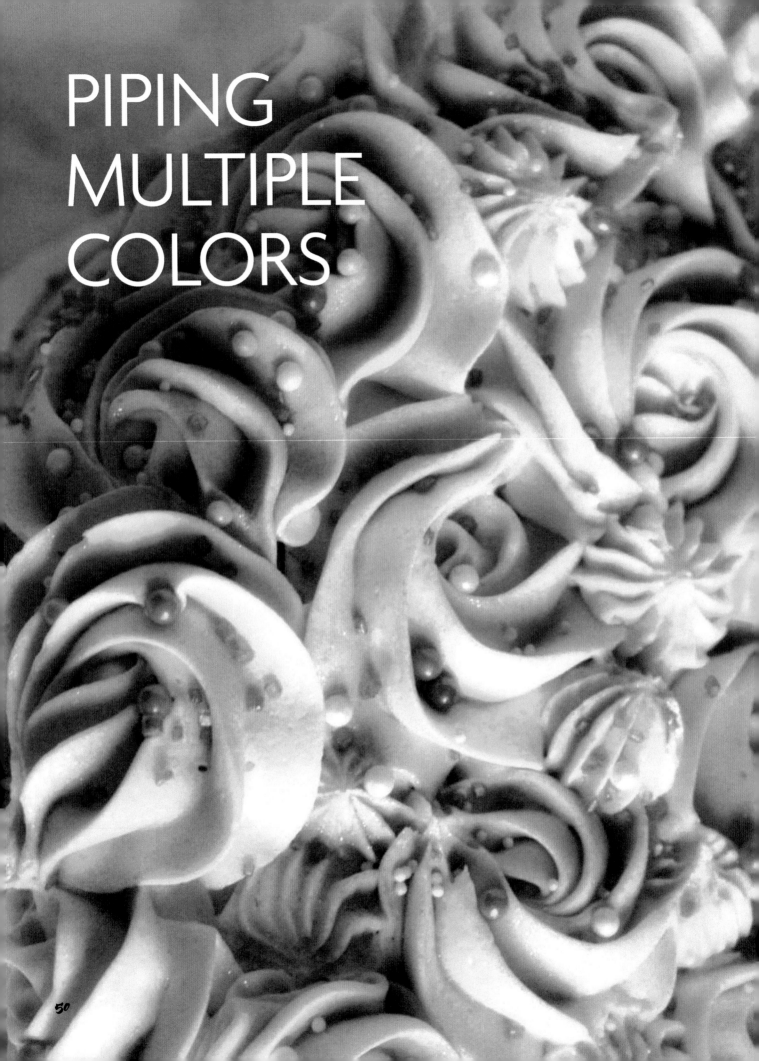

PIPING MULTIPLE COLORS

STEP 1

Lay out a large piece of plastic wrap. Prepare multiple colors of frosting and place each frosting in a piping bag. Cut off the tip of the piping bag. Pipe one line of buttercream on the plastic wrap with the first color.

STEP 2

Pipe the next color in a straight line following the first. You can pipe as many colored lines as you want to come through when you pipe. If you have more colors, pipe thinner lines so that they will all fit in your piping bag and come through at the same time.

STEP 3

Fold over your piping bag so that the first color touches the last color.

STEP 4

Roll the plastic wrap together like a burrito and twist one end.

STEP 5

Cut the other end of your plastic wrap so that the colors can easily be piped out.

STEP 6

Place the plastic wrapped buttercream inside your piping bag that is already prepared with your tip. I'm using a 1M tip here. (I have also used a 4B French tip.)

STEP 7

Do a couple practice pipes on a plate to make sure all the colors are coming through before piping it on to your cake or cupcakes.

QUICK & EASY
FANCY
CUPCAKES

1M **2D**

Here are the three different tips that I use when piping "rosettes" on either cupcakes or the side of a cake. The 1M, 1B, & 2D all work very well. The one I'm using today is the 1B.

STEP 1

Start by piping in the middle of your cupcake. Pipe right above the cupcake and not against it. Use your pressure on the bag to pipe the icing out.

STEP 2

Swirl your tip around the center, keeping constant pressure on your bag and a constant flow of buttercream. *If you drag your icing around the cupcake rather than let it flow out above your cupcake, it will look more flat and not full.*

STEP 3

Continue the pressure on your piping bag until you have swirled all around your beginning center.

STEP 4

Release the pressure on your piping bag but keep pulling in the same motion to end the swirl.

STEP 5

Add the sprinkles! I used regular and tiny sized sugar pearls. If you're using a crusting buttercream, like my (mock) American buttercream, then you'll only want to pipe about three cupcakes at a time and then add the sprinkles. This is so that you've added the sprinkles before the buttercream starts to crust, otherwise the sprinkles will not stick to the buttercream.

PIPING A
BASKET
WEAVE

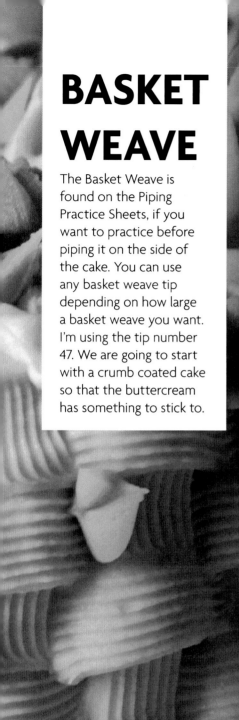

BASKET WEAVE

The Basket Weave is found on the Piping Practice Sheets, if you want to practice before piping it on the side of the cake. You can use any basket weave tip depending on how large a basket weave you want. I'm using the tip number 47. We are going to start with a crumb coated cake so that the buttercream has something to stick to.

STEP 1

First, you will pipe a straight line up using continuous pressure until you reach the top.

STEP 2

Starting a little bit before your line, pipe straight across it, overlapping it on both sides. You will leave a gap the size of your tip in between each line.

STEP 3

Pipe straight up vertically again, overlapping the ones you just piped across but leaving a small gap between the last vertical line and this one.

STEP 4

Fill the gaps by piping horizontal lines again, straight across and overlapping your previous vertical line.

STEP 5

Repeat again by piping the next vertical line straight down, covering the tails of the last horizontal lines.

STEP 6

Continue weaving your basket all the way around your cake.

THE ROPE

The Rope can be used as a border around the top and bottom of your cake. When making flower basket cakes, I especially like the rope to look like it ties together my basket on both the top and bottom borders of my cake.

(This basically looks like a sideways S.)

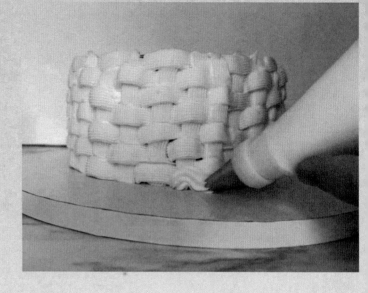

STEP 1

Repeat again by piping the next vertical line straight down, covering the tails of the last horizontal lines.

STEP 4

On top of your cake you're also going to pipe a rope, but you're going to switch the direction of your piping. Pipe straight down instead of the side.

STEP 5

Keeping on the edge of your cake, pipe the rope all the way around the top.

Your buttercream basket is complete! It's now ready to add flowers. If you want to add the flowers that look like these, you can check out the Russian Piping Tips in the buttercream flowers section. You can also add any of the flowers from that section. The possibilities are endless!

STEP 2

In the curve of your last S pipe the next s.

STEP 3

Continue piping S until you reach all around your cake.

PIPE A
BUTTERCREAM SCARF

Using the X motion that can be practiced on the Piping Practice Sheets, you can pipe a buttercream scarf on the side of the cake. You can use a fully frosted cake or just crumb coated cake. You'll be adding plenty of buttercream on the cake by piping the scarf so it's really only necessary to crumb coat the sides of the cake. You will however, at least want a crumb coat so that your piping has something to stick to.

STEP 1

Use a rolling pin to crush your graham crackers in your plastic bag.

STEP 2

Starting at the top, pipe down at an angle.

STEP 3

Pipe the next shell right next to the first, only pull down in the opposite direction so that the two tails overlap when meeting.

STEP 4

Follow the steps of the X that we used on the Piping Practice Sheet, slightly staggering your X as you pipe your line of buttercream X's.

STEP 5

When you pipe the next line of Xs, fit your X in the space created by the last line.

STEP 6

You can switch out colors for your scarf and make whatever pattern you want. I piped three lines and then switched colors.

STEP 7

When you reach the end of the scarf, pipe a row of shells, coming in horizontally.

STEP 8

Finally create the tassels by piping both colors out horizontally in the opposite direction.

OMBRE
ROSETTE CAKE

STEP 1

Starting with a freshly crumb coated cake (not chilled because we want the rosettes to stick to our cake and not fall off later), mark where you want to place your layers of rosettes. You can use a cake marker like this Wilton one or tape toothpicks to a ruler and use that. I give about an inch and a half for each rosette swirl. I let my top rosette line have room to build onto the top of the cake so that one can be less than an inch.

STEP 2

Starting with your darkest color, use your Wilton 1M tip to pipe the first rosette. Placing your 1M tip in the middle of your first marked line, pipe around the center and continue to pipe until the tail comes out to the side. Keep the rosette between your first line.

STEP 3

Pipe the next rosette beginning on the tail of the last one. Continue piping rosettes all around the cake. Make sure you slightly overlap each rosette so you don't have gaps.

STEP 4

For the next line of rosettes, take a heaping tablespoon of your previous color and double the amount of white buttercream. Mix them together to create your next rosette color.

STEP 5

Pipe the next row of rosettes, beginning in the middle of that marked row and keeping that rosette in between the two bottom ones.

STEP 6

Using the color you just finished piping, mix it with the white to create your next row of colors. You'll do this each time. You need a shade lighter for each line of rosettes.

STEP 7

On the top row, allow your rosette to pipe up and over the top and then come down to finish your rosette.

STEP 8

Your top rows of rosettes will not fit exactly in between each rosette of the previous row. Just make sure they slightly overlap so you don't have gaps.

STEP 9

The final rosette should be in the center of your cake.

BUTTERCREAM
MARBLING

Tools you'll need: Several different shades of buttercream, off-set spatula, acetate (or wax paper), sharp knife, & scissors.

For the highlighting, I used Rose Gold sterling dust from the Sugar Art store.

I used dusty rose Americolor gel food coloring to color the buttercream.

Note: I used acetate (for baking), also known as cake collars, to apply the buttercream to the cake with. You can also use wax paper, like I did for the black and white cake. The pros and cons of wax paper is that it has a smoother finish but is more flimsy and difficult to apply to a cake. Acetate is easier to apply to a cake but has a more textured finish than the wax paper.

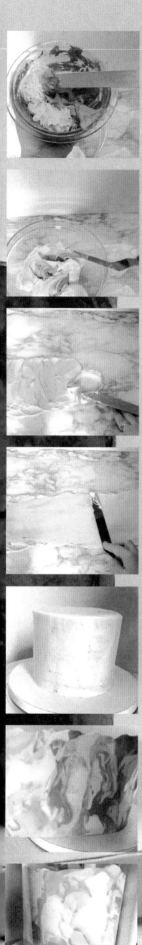

STEP 1

Scoop two or three shades of buttercream onto your off-set spatula.

STEP 2

Gently fold these colors into your primary color (mine was white so that the colors would show up well). Caution: do not mix your colors otherwise they will be too blended and not give you the marbled affect. You really only want to turn them over a couple times.

STEP 3

Using your off-set spatula, scoop the marbled colors and press them onto your acetate, gently pressing your spatula back and forth on the acetate. The colors on the side facing you will be blended but the other side will look marbled. Make sure you get all the way to the bottom and estimate how high the cake you need to cover is (it's better to go higher rather than shorter because we'll be trimming the top later) Note: I have placed my acetate down on a piece of wax paper so I don't make a mess on my table.

STEP 4

Even out the buttercream with your off-set spatula.

STEP 5

Use a freshly crumb coated cake so that the buttercream will stick to it and not fall off later.

STEP 6

Pick up your acetate from both ends, holding it tight. Make sure the bottom is straight against the bottom of your cake.

STEP 7

Smooth and press the acetate into your cake using a fondant smoother or your hand if you don't have one.

STEP 8

Use your scissors to cut the excess acetate from your cake.

STEP 9

Smooth it once more with your fondant smoother or hand.

STEP 10

Place your cake in the freezer for 45 minutes. Gently peel the acetate from your cake.

STEP 11

Heat your sharp knife with a blow torch. You can also dip it in boiling water and wipe off the water with a paper towel.

STEP 12

Slice the excess buttercream off along the top of your cake. You can go straight across or use a more rough stone cut look by going up and down with your hand as you go around.

STEP 13

Using an edible dust like Sugar Art's Sterling Pearl rose gold color, make it into paint using a few drops of alcohol or something like a vanilla extract that contains alcohol. The alcohol will evaporate.

STEP 14

Paint the top edge of your cake and any other accents using a food safe paint brush and your luster dust mixture.

WAVES & SCALES
BEACH THEMED CAKE

Tools you'll need: Ateco 808 large writing tip, Wilton 1M tip, pale blue and green buttercream, and graham crackers in ziploc bag.

STEP 1

Use a rolling pin to crush your graham crackers in your plastic bag.

STEP 2

When the graham crackers are finely crushed, pour them on the top of a crumb coated cake.

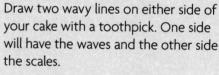

STEP 3

Smooth the graham crackers all around the top of your cake. Make sure you cover the top of your cake all the way to the edges.

STEP 4

Draw two wavy lines on either side of your cake with a toothpick. One side will have the waves and the other side the scales.

STEP 5

Pipe on the scales with your Ateco 808 tip and green buttercream. Starting at the bottom, pipe a dot, releasing pressure on your bag, press into your dot with your tip and drag your tip to the side. Pipe the next dot on the tail of the previous dot.

STEP 6

Use the Wilton 1M tip and blue buttercream for the waves. At the bottom of the cake, pipe a rosette with a swish up. Continue piping around the starting point, and end with a swish up.

STEP 7

Dip the sprinkles in a tiny bit of fresh buttercream, applying them to the side of the cake. The fresh buttercream will act as your glue. I use a pair of tweezers that I have set aside for cake decorating to apply my sprinkles.

65

Tools you'll need: White and black candy melts, silicone baking mat or parchment paper, clothes pins or mini clamps, wooden skewer

STEP 1

Melt the candy melts in the microwave at 30 second intervals, mixing them between each interval until they are smooth.

STEP 2

On your silicone baking mat or parchment paper, pour several large stripes of the white candy melts.

STEP 3

Pour smaller amounts of the black candy melts between each of the white stripes.

STEP 4

Use your wooden skewer to swirl the two colors, giving it a marbled look.

STEP 5

Fold the silicone mat or parchment paper in two spots while the candy melts are still soft and clamp them in place with clothes pins or mini clamps.

STEP 6

Once the candy melts have completely hardened, gently peel it from the silicone mat or parchment paper. Take care that you don't snap it.

STEP 7

Gently press it down into the top of your cake. I add a little bit of extra buttercream around the back to glue it in place.

Optional: You can paint the edges with edible silver Diamondust (from SugarArt.com) made into a paint with a little clear vanilla extract or vodka (the alcohol will evaporate as it dries). I apply it with a food safe paint brush like Wilton's.

You can also use black food coloring like I used on this one. I also sprinkled it with the silver Diamondust and added edible silver flakes. There are so many different options!

RICE PAPER SAILS

Tools you'll need: Rice paper (spring roll or Vietnamese egg roll paper), lollipop sticks, or wooden skewers, gel food coloring, silicone mat or waxed paper, clips, pans of cool water, and gloves.

Optional for shimmer and highlights: Silver "Diamondust" pump, silver sterling pearl dust, (both of those can be found at thesugarart.com), food-safe paint brush, and some kind of alcohol to thin it. Some vanilla extracts have alcohol or you can use vodka. The alcohol will evaporate.

STEP 1

Clip your silicone mat or wax paper into small folds resembling an accordion when you're done.

STEP 2

Place your rice paper into a pan of cool water. Let it sit for about a minute.

STEP 3

Drop a drip of gel food coloring into the water and give it another 30 seconds or so. If you want solid color sails simply drop in the gel food coloring before the rice paper and mix it in the water. The sails we're making will have color splashes. I used three different colors of blue in each of my pans: royal blue, electric blue, and sky blue.

STEP 4

Pull up your rice paper and drape it over your silicone mat.

STEP 5

Using a lollipop stick, place it half on the end of your sail and twist it in. Right now it will be loose, but it will stick when it dries.

STEP 6

Using the silver Diamondust pump, pump the dust all over the sail.

STEP 7

Apply silver sterling pearl dust with a paint brush to the edges and certain accents after using a tiny bit of alcohol, like vodka, to turn it into a paint.

STEP 8

You can create an extra tall sail by simply layering the rice paper sails.

STEP 9

Allow the rice paper to air dry over night.

STEP 10

Slowly peel the rice paper sails from the silicone mat.

STEP 11

Strategically place your sails on the cake while pressing your sticks down into the cake.

Advanced Cake Decorating

This might be a section of the book that intimidates you. You may just plan to have fun browsing through it. Either way is okay! But I also hope that by doing some of the simpler techniques from other sections, you will be able to build up your confidence to create some really sculptural, gravity defying, or highly detailed cake masterpieces- if that's your goal.

Start small. Maybe take different, more basic elements from some of the more advanced structures, and work them into your own vision. Nobody becomes an expert at anything overnight.

Making cake art is just like any other skill. You just need to keep practicing. If I can do it, you can do it too! (And no matter what it looks like, Elaina will eat it!)

CAKE WITH
BUTTERCREAM STRIPES &
CHOCOLATE DRIP &
ANTI-GRAVITY POURING

It's three for the price of one! Though clearly, you are welcome to mix and match these skills (as well as any others from this book or elsewhere) to suit your cake vision. Get crazy!

BUTTERCREAM STRIPES

Tools you'll need: Two different colors of buttercream (I used peanut butter and chocolate), cake comb, bench scraper, off-set spatula, and a pastry bag.

STEP 1

Smooth your first color over your cake. Use a cake comb that has wide gaps like this one.

STEP 2

Press the comb into your cake with the bottom touching your cake board and your comb at a 90 degree angle. Keep scraping the buttercream all the way around your cake, removing the buttercream from your comb as you go. Stop after you have deep wells in your buttercream but don't go so far that you touch the actual cake and start getting crumbs in your buttercream.

STEP 3

Fill your pastry bag with your second buttercream color. Cut a small hole in your piping bag. Pipe the second color buttercream in all your wells. Having your cake on a turntable really helps this process.

STEP 4

Use your bench scraper to smooth both stripes together. Fill in any gaps if needed with that color buttercream. If your lines look too blurry, dip your bench scraper in hot water, wipe off the water with a paper towel, and scrape until the lines are sharp and smooth.

STEP 5

Knock down and pull inward with your off-set spatula to smooth the top of your cake.

Tip: A chocolate drip is a great way to finish a cake with stripes! You could also incorporate a border of some sort, or keep it smooth.

ANTI-GRAVITY POURING

Tools you'll need: Mini chocolate chips (you can also use regular chocolate chips), bendable smoothie straw (I used my cake frame, but a bendable smoothie straw works just as well), skewer, candy (I used mini peanut butter cups).

STEP 1

Put the chocolate chips in the microwave, stirring at 30 second intervals until melted. Insert the skewer into your straw for support and press it into your cake, leaving the bendable part on top.

STEP 2

Coat your straw with the melted chocolate. This will act as our glue for the candy.

STEP 3

Starting at the bottom of the straw, press your candy into the chocolate. Work your way up the straw covering it with candy.

At the base I placed whole peanut butter cups and then cut the rest in half and pressed them onto my straw, working my way up to the bend. You can use lots of different kinds of candy for this method so the fun is limitless! Reapply the chocolate as needed if it starts to dry.

STEP 4

At the top, I taped a bag right at the bend so that the top part of my straw was taped to the inside of the bag.

CHOCOLATE DRIP

Tools you'll need: Mini chocolate chips (you can also use regular chocolate chips or white chocolate chips), water, pastry bag, off-set spatula.
You will want a 3:1 ratio of liquid to chocolate chips. You can use water, milk, or heavy cream. A little over 3 oz water to 10 oz mini chocolate chips.

STEP 1

Put the chocolate chips in the microwave for 30 seconds. (They will just be slightly warm but not melted.)

STEP 2

Simmer your liquid. Pour the hot liquid over the warm chocolate chips, making sure that it covers all your chocolate chips as much as possible. Let it rest for 5 minutes. This will allow it to continue it's melting process.

Note: If you were using white chocolate chips and wanted to make a colored drip, like the ice cream cone cake, mix in gel food coloring to your hot liquid before adding it to the chocolate.

STEP 3

After it has sat in the hot liquid for 5 minutes, use your whisk to thoroughly whisk your chocolate until all the lumps are gone and the chocolate is smooth. If you still have some lumps, place the bowl in the microwave for 30 seconds and then whisk again.

Let your chocolate cool to about 90 degrees or slightly warmer than room temperature. This is very important otherwise your drips will be too runny. Make sure the cake that you are pouring it on has been well-chilled in the fridge.

STEP 4

Pour your chocolate over the top of your cake almost to the edges.

STEP 5

Smooth it with your off-set spatula while the chocolate is still warm.

STEP 6

Prepare a pastry bag by folding it over a cup to hold it open and pour the remaining chocolate into the bag. Cut the tip of the bag, and use it to control where you place your drips on the cake. The longer you pipe in one place, the longer your drips will be. I like to have a good mix of long and short drips so I send longer in certain spots than others.

CHOCOLATE BOWL

Tools you'll need: Mini chocolate chips (you can also use regular chocolate chips), pastry bag, ice bowl.

I made my ice bowl by using half of my 6-inch ball cake pan, but you can use any bowl that you can put in the freezer to make your bowl. Fill it with water and leave it overnight. I dipped my pan in warm water to easily remove my ice bowl. Place the ice bowl on a piece of wax paper, on a folded towel, and place that on your turntable. You can do it without a turntable, but I just found it super easy with one.

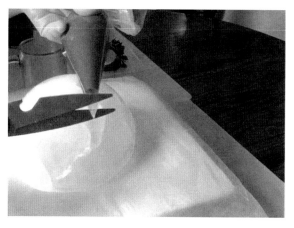

STEP 1

Put the chocolate chips in the microwave, stirring at 30 second intervals until melted. Fold your pastry bag in half over a cup and then pour the chocolate in.

STEP 2

Cut off the tip of the pastry bag.

STEP 3

Starting in the middle of your bowl, use a lowercase "e" motion to loop chocolate in overlapping loops around your bowl. You can really use any design when creating your bowl as long as the design all overlaps.

STEP 4

Continue piping loops of chocolate until your ice bowl is covered. You may want to make a flat area on what will be the bowl base to assure it sits better.

STEP 5

Wait a few minutes for your chocolate to harden before lifting it off the bowl.

If you're placing the bowl on a drip cake, use a little bit of fresh chocolate to anchor it in place. If you're placing the bowl on a buttercream cake, you can use a little bit of fresh buttercream on the cake to glue it in place. Then have fun filling your bowl with yummy things! I used chocolate covered strawberries.

BUTTERFLY
BLING

Tools you'll need: Piping tip Ateco 124, large round tip, Sweetapolita's Pinball blend of metallic sprinkles, food-safe tweezers.

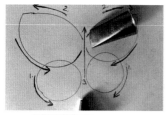

STEP 1

Use a toothpick to mark off where you want to place your butterfly's body.

STEP 2

Using the Ateco 124 tip, with the narrow end facing up toward the center of the body, pipe the round rear wings of the butterfly by pivoting your hand in a half circle as you apply pressure to your bag.

STEP 3

The narrow end of your tip will always be on the outside of the wing and will be facing the opposite direction when you're done pivoting. Release the pressure on your bag and pull your tip in.

STEP 4

Repeat the steps for the other side.

STEP 5

For the long wings, start at the top of your butterfly's body with the 124 tip facing towards the top of the butterfly, and pipe an angled line.

STEP 6

Pivot and pipe the line back in toward the body of your butterfly with the 124 tip now facing down towards the rear of your butterfly. Your long wings will overlap your small wings.

STEP 7

Using a large round tip, pipe the butterfly's head first by applying pressure to your piping bag and letting the dot build. Next, pipe the body by piping a line straight down the butterfly's body.

STEP 8

Use your tweezers to place some metallic rod sprinkles on the butterfly's wings. Always dip your sprinkles in fresh buttercream before placing them so that they will stick. Fresh buttercream will act as your glue.

STEP 9

Pipe on your butterfly's antenna.

STEP 10

Place some triangular sprinkles on the ends.

STEP 11

Create a trail of sprinkles for your butterfly using the round sprinkles. I used some of the larger balls closer to the butterfly and then the small ones trailing away from the butterfly.

STEP 12

Pipe two color lines of buttercream on plastic wrap and then fold it over like a burrito. Twist one end and cut off the other end and place that end into your piping bag prepared with a large open star tip. (This is the pipe multiple colors method that we did in the basics section.)

STEP 13

Around the top edge of your cake use an "e" motion to pipe the border. This is the same motion that we used on our "piping practice sheet" only using a larger tip.

STEP 14

Sprinkle the border with more Sweetapolita sprinkles.

FLOWER POT
CAKE

*Edible tools you'll need: Giant
cupcake (cooled), Chocolate
buttercream , Vanilla buttercream (using
Americolors Leaf green mixed with Forest Green), Buttercream
roses that you have piped and set in the freezer to harden
using Americolors Dusty Rose to color stripe your bag.*

*Other tools you'll need: Decorating tips (366, 2B, 3,
Ateco 124), Serrated knife, Off set spatula*

STEP 1

First allow your giant cupcake to fully cool.

STEP 2

Next smooth your chocolate buttercream over the bottom half of the giant cupcake. Using your #2B decorating tip, pipe a rim around the top to look like a flow pot.

STEP 3

Trim off the peak of the top of your cupcake.

STEP 4

Apply a rough crumb coat of green buttercream.

STEP 5

Take your Korean buttercream roses out of the freezer and press them on to the top.

STEP 6

Pipe some green buds using your #3 decorating tip.

STEP 7

Pipe pale pink buds on top of the green ones using a piping bag with a small tip cut out.

STEP 8

Fill in the rest of the pot with green leaves using your tip #366.

BUTTERCREAM TRANSFER
STAINED GLASS CAKE

STEP 1

Draw and measure several panels for your buttercream transfer. I used 3 for this size cake. You can also draw a sketch of your stained glass window here or print a coloring book page from the internet.

STEP 2

Tape your drawing down to a piece of cardboard. Place a piece of wax paper over it and trace the exact picture with black buttercream. Pop it in the freezer for 5 minutes to firm up.

STEP 3

Make various colors of buttercream for your stained glass.

Buttercream transfers are an amazing way to put the image that you want, with buttercream, on a cake. The image can be small or large and be placed on the top or sides of your cake. You can print off an image from online to be your template to trace with buttercream, or you can draw your own! In this tutorial, I'll show you a large buttercream transfer that's measured to fit exactly around the circumference of your cake.

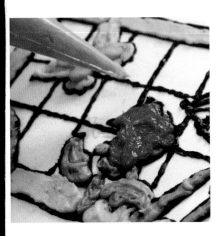

STEP 4

Fill in each section with the buttercream color of your choice. Press the buttercream down as you go so that it will be smooth on the other side. Pop it in the freezer between colors that will be touching.

STEP 5

Like the back of a tapestry, as you add your colors, it will look muddled on this side. When it's time to flip over, you'll reveal your beautiful image.

STEP 6

After popping it in the freezer for about 20 minutes to firm up, smooth a thin layer of buttercream across it all to connect it all and even it out. Then pop it back in the freezer for 30 minutes.

STEP 7

Smooth buttercream on your cake before getting your panels out of the freezer.

STEP 8

Press the buttercream panel onto your freshly iced cake. Smooth it with your fondant smoother.

STEP 9

Gently peel off the wax paper.

STEP 10

Touch up any buttercream as needed.

STEP 11

Pipe a buttercream border around the top. Place your pulled sugar rose on top of your cake.

First you'll need to build a cake structure. Here are two options for you:

Option one: (This is the one I used this time.) You will need a cake frame with floating plates. I bought a Lehao brand from Amazon. They are not super sturdy so you're not going to want to move the cake after assembly. For a more sturdy structure, choose option two.

Option two:
Build your own PVC structure. You will need at least an inch-thick wooden cake board for a base, 1/2 inch PVC pipe, coupling slip and a threaded adapter for the 1/2 inch PVC pipe, drill, PVC pipe cutter, 6 inch round wooden cake board, and 7/8 inch spade bit, to make the hole. You will also need a floor flange (like the ones we used in the Assemble a Cake Structure tutorial),

and wood screws. Use your wood screws to attach your floor flange to the middle of your wooden cake board. Thread the PVC adapter into the floor flange and place the 1/2 inch PVC pipe in this. Measure how long you want your cone of your cake and cut the PVC pipe here. Fit the PVC coupling slip on top of this section. Use your 7/8 inch spade bit to drill a hole in your 6 inch round wooden cake circle. After making the cone in step one, place the wooden cake circle on top of the coupling slip and thread another length of the PVC pipe through the 6 inch wooden cake circle and press it into the coupling slip. The cake will be completely held up and supported by the coupling slip. It will give the illusion that the ice cream cone is holding up the entire cake but it's really this coupling slip that supports the whole

cake that will rest on the suspended cake board. To break it down, the structure itself will look like two long pieces of PVC pipe divided by the coupling slip with the wooden cake board suspended in the middle. Use an apple corer to create a hole in the center of the cakes and thread them through the PVC pipe when it's time to stack the cakes. You can omit the smoothie straw step because the PVC pipe will act as the stabilizer for the cakes instead of the smoothie straws. This structure will be the most stable of the two and easier to transport a cake.

ICE CREAM CONE
CAKE

Tools you'll need: Three 6 inch dome cakes (I used the Wilton ball cake pan), turntable, 12 oz puffed rice cereal, 16 oz mini marshmallows, 4 oz candy melts or chocolate, gloves, shortening, quilted imprint mat, 11 oz white chocolate chips, 6 oz semi sweet chocolate chips, off-set spatula, flexible cake scraper, serrated knife, buttercream, gel food coloring, 1M tip, 6 inch round cardboard cake circle with a hole in the center, 3 smoothie straws, and a wooden skewer.

STEP 1

Measure how tall you want your cone and make the center support that length. In a large bowl warm about 12 oz of your mini marshmallows in the microwave at 30 second intervals, mixing between each interval until the marshmallows are all melted. Melt the candy melts or chocolate in the same way. Add the puffed rice cereal, marshmallows, and the candy melts together and mix well. Melt the remaining marshmallows in the microwave. Rub shortening all over your gloves to keep the marshmallows from sticking to them. Cover the support with melted marshmallows.

STEP 2

Firmly press your puffed rice cereal mixture into the center support forming a thick cone. Make sure the top of the cone will be wide enough to fit your 6 inch cake dome.

STEP 3

Wrap the cone with plastic wrap and keep it in the fridge overnight.

STEP 4

Use your serrated knife to sculpt your cone, taking care that the top of the cone remains 6 inches round.

STEP 5

Use an offset spatula to smooth ganache onto your cone and then scrape smooth with a flexible cake scraper.

Here's how I made my ganache for this cone. In a bowl add an 11 oz. bag of white chocolate chips and about 6 oz. of semi-sweet chocolate chips. Place it in the microwave for 30 seconds. Cover the chocolate chips with 4 oz. of simmering hot water. Let stand for 5 minutes. Add a drop of orange gel food coloring and whisk the chocolate until smooth. If it's still lumpy, place it in the microwave for 30 seconds and whisk again. Set it aside until completely cool (about 4 hours).

STEP 6

Use your scraper to make a diagonal line in the cone. This will give it more of the look of a waffle cone.

STEP 7

Chill the cone for about 20 minutes for the chocolate to be not as sticky. Press the quilted imprint mat onto the cone. You will need to press it into one section and then move it to the next section and press it into that one, until the whole cone looks quilted.

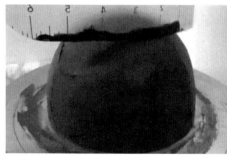

STEP 8

Place the first cake dome on the 6 inch round cardboard cake circle, using buttercream to stick it to the cardboard. Place this on your turntable. Cover the dome with buttercream using a piping bag and then smooth it out with a flexible cake scraper. Place the cake in the freezer for 30 minutes so that you can pick it up easier and place it on the cone later.

Note: For a simpler one scoop ice cream cone, you can omit the next two dome layers. I enjoy living life on the edge, so we'll continue on with the triple scoop ice cream cone.

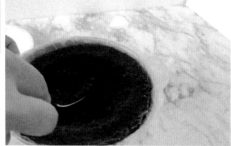

STEP 9

The next two domes will need to have part of their center scooped out in order to fit on to the first. (They will fit together like scoops of ice cream when assembled.) It's essentially a 3 layer cake with each layer being thick. I placed plastic wrap in my pans that I used to bake the cakes and then placed the cakes back in there. This kept them in place while I was scooping out the middle.

STEP 10

Pipe buttercream into the domes and scrape them off like a semi naked cake. This step will keep the crumbs from falling onto your cakes when you stack them. Chill it in the fridge for 20 minutes.

STEP 11

Flip both of your scooped, chilled cake domes over onto a cardboard circle to frost.

STEP 12

Cover both domes with buttercream using your piping bag. Smooth them using your flexible cake scraper. Place them in the freezer for 30 minutes.

STEP 13

Decorate your cake board by smoothing buttercream over the board. Scoop sprinkles on to the board and smooth them out until the cake board is completely covered in sprinkles. Next, pat them in gently.

STEP 14

Place your support at the top of your cone, and then place your plate on this. The cake should be supported by the support that comes in your kit. None of the pressure should be on your rice cereal cone.

STEP 15

Apply some buttercream to your cake plate to help be the glue to stick your cake to the plate. Remove the first cake dome from the freezer. This one was the solid dome. Work your bench scraper or offset spatula under the cake, all the way around, to help lift it onto the plate on your cone.

STEP 16

Pipe a dollop of buttercream on top of that cake.

STEP 17

Remove your next cake from the freezer and again use your bench scraper or off-set spatula to assist lifting your cake onto the first cake. Gently press the cake onto the first cake. You can clean up any blemishes you created with your flexible cake scraper.

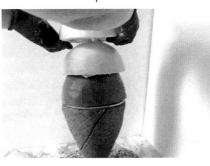

REPEAT STEPS 16 & 17 FOR THE FINAL LAYER

Note: If you used option two cake structure, you can skip steps 19 & 20 because your PVC pipe has already threaded your cakes and is your stabilizer.

STEP 18

Press a wooden skewer down the middle to anchor all the cakes together.

STEP 19

Measure and cut three smoothie straws to the size of your cakes. Press them into the top of your cakes evenly spaced around the wood skewer. These will help stabilize and anchor your cakes together.

STEP 20

Use your 1M tip and with a gentle U motion of your wrist pipe a ruffly border around each scoop.

STEP 21

Drip a chocolate drip on top of your cake using the chocolate drip method that we learned in the Chocolate Drip tutorial.

STEP 22

Pipe a little white buttercream on top of your ice cream cone, using the 1M tip, to look like whip cream.

STEP 23

Add sprinkles and a cherry, and your cake is done!

This may seem like a daunting task. There are many different kinds of structures, but a PVC pipe structure is one of my favorites because of the versatility and the ease of use. It essentially fits together like a 3D puzzle. There are so many different structures you can build once you have the main piece attached to the board. You can easily remove and readjust the PVC pipes to have a central attachment instead of two legs to use for a different structure; I'll be showing you how to build the Standing Figure Structure.

ASSEMBLING A
CAKE STRUCTURE

Tools you'll need: Drill, Phillips head drill bit, 7/8 inch spade bit, PVC cutter, ruler

Other materials needed: inch thick wooden board for the base, 5 & 4 inch round wooden cake boards, 2 floor flanges (galvanized), wood screws #12 x 3/4 inch, & contact paper

The PVC pipe and fittings all need to be for the 1/2 inch thick PVC pipe. You'll need: 1/2 inch thick PVC pipe, (2) PVC pipe adapters (slip x threaded), (4) 90 degree elbow slip (socket x spigot), Tee Slip, 4 way adapter slip, (2) 45 degree elbow slip, (2) coupling (slip)

At the very top of my structure I used an additional 90 degree elbow slip (socket x spigot) because my figure will have a ponytail.

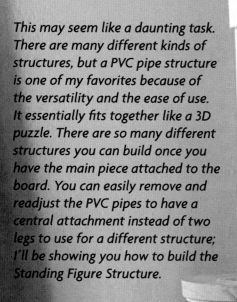

STEP 1

First cover your cake board with contact paper so that it is easy to wipe down and is reusable.

STEP 2

Measure where you want the feet to stand on your base. Using your drill, with the Phillips head attachment and wood screws, secure your floor flanges to your base.

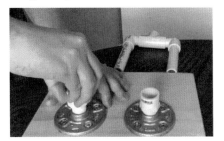

STEP 3

Twist in your PVC pipe threaded adapters into the floor flanges.

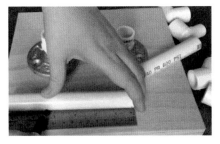

STEP 4

Measure out how long you need the ½-inch thick PVC for the figure's legs, body, and arms of your structure. (The lengths will vary depending on what kind of figure you are making.)

STEP 5

Use your PVC pipe cutters to cut the marked pipes.

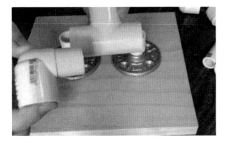

STEP 6

Use the 90 degree elbow slip (socket x spigot) to attach the PVC pipes to the Tee Slip.

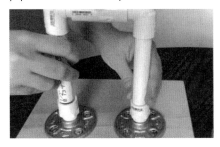

STEP 7

The 1/2 inch thick PVC pipes can then be inserted into your adapters.

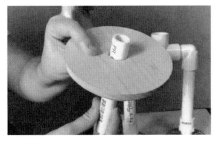

STEP 8

Drill a hole in the middle of your 5 and 4 inch round wooden boards using your 7/8-inch spade bit. (Your boards don't need to be as thick as mine. They just need to be sturdy enough to support your cake.)

STEP 9

The hole created with this spade bit will create a hole large enough for the 1/2 inch thick PVC pipe to be threaded through it but small enough that it will rest above your attachments.

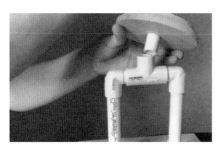

STEP 10

Insert a length of your 1/2 inch PVC pipe through the hole of your 5 inch round cake board and press the pipe into the top of your Tee Slip.

STEP 11

Press the 4 way adapter on top of that. Insert another length of your 1/2 inch PVC pipe through your 4 inch round cake board and press the pipe into the top of your 4 way adapter slip.

STEP 12

Create the arms. Each arm will have these pieces in this order, starting at one side of the four way adapter slip: one inch length of your PVC pipe, 45 degree elbow slip, one inch length of your PVC pipe, 90 degree elbow slip (socket x spigot), & coupling slip.

At the very top of mine, I also used a 45 degree (socket x spigot) to support the "pony tail" of my figure.

Before placing your cake on the structure, cover your floor flanges with foil to keep it all food safe.

CONSTRUCTING A
STANDING
FIGURE

Using the cake structure for a standing figure, you can begin this cake. Cover the round cake boards in foil for easier clean up. I baked my cakes in a 6 inch Wilton ball cake pan, three 5 inch round cakes, and one mini cupcake. The legs and arms we will make from puffed rice cereal treats and the entire figure is covered in buttercream. Cakes should always be chilled in the fridge before carving.

ARMS & LEGS

Tools you'll need: 12 oz puffed rice cereal, 16 oz mini marshmallows, 4 oz candy melts or chocolate, gloves, shortening.

STEP 1

In a large bowl, warm about 12 oz of your mini marshmallows in the microwave at 30 second intervals, mixing between each interval until the marshmallows are all melted. Melt the candy melts or chocolate in the same way. Add the puffed rice cereal, melted marshmallows, and the candy melts together and mix well.

STEP 2

Melt the remaining marshmallows in the microwave. Rub shortening all over your gloves to keep the marshmallows from sticking to them. Cover the arms, legs, and under the cake board with melted marshmallows.

STEP 3

Firmly press your puffed rice cereal mixture into the legs and arms until you reach the size you want. It's better to go a little bigger because you can trim off the excess later. Wrap the legs and arms with plastic wrap and place in the fridge overnight.

STEP 4

Using a serrated knife trim your figure's legs and arms to the desired size.

BODY

Tools you'll need: Three 5 inch round cakes, buttercream, pastry bag, flexible plastic cake scraper, apple corer, offset spatula

STEP 1

Lift off the arm portion of the cake structure and set it aside.

STEP 2

Measure how tall you need the body to be and level the cakes to the correct size. Next, stack them and cut a hole down the middle using an apple corer.

STEP 3

Thread the cakes down PVC structure one at a time, smoothing buttercream between each layer by piping it on with a pastry bag and smoothing it with your off-set spatula.

STEP 4

Line up the arm structure to the PVC pipe, pressing the two pipes together so that your structure securely fits together.

STEP 5

Carve the body of your cake with a serrated knife to the desired size. You should always use chilled cakes when carving.

STEP 6

Apply buttercream all over the body, arms, and legs.

STEP 7

Smooth it out with a flexible plastic cake scraper. I like using flexible cake scrapers anytime that I have to scrape something that is curved because you can flex and curve your cake scraper to the desired shape.

Note: I do a section at a time so that I can smooth the buttercream before it crusts. I started with the chest, piped the buttercream on and then smoothed it. Next, I did the front of the legs and then moved on to the back sections until my whole cake was covered and scraped.

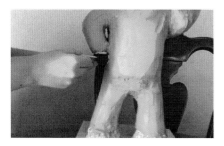

STEP 8

Secure your mini cupcake, for the hand, right under the arm and to the side of your cake using a bit of buttercream and a wooden skewer.

STEP 9

Pipe on the buttercream details on your cake. Smooth details like the hand with your flexible cake scraper.

HEAD

STEP 1

Carve one of your 6 inch domes (from your 6 inch ball cake), trimming off the top so that it is the same size as your 4 inch wooden cake board. (One of the reasons I used a 4 inch wooden plaque for my structure was because I liked the shape of the plaque for the head. You can find wooden plaques at Michael's or on Amazon) Set aside everything that you trim off into a separate bowl that we will use soon.

STEP 2

This is the bottom half of your head that we will be flipping soon. Use your serrated knife to trim it so that it narrows more at the base where your board is.

STEP 3

Set the board aside and flip over your cake. Place your second 6 inch dome on top of it after applying buttercream between them. Use your apple corer to make your hole through the head.

STEP 4

Apply buttercream to your cake board and place your cake on it. I use a larger cardboard circle to place my whole cake on so I have something to carry it on when I place it in the fridge later. Shape your cake by carving it with your serrated knife.

STEP 6

Using the cake pieces that we've set aside, break it apart into small crumbs, add about a tablespoon or two of buttercream and mix it together using your hand or a hand mixer. The mixture in this bowl will be a very sticky cake pop consistency. Scoop out some of this mixture and press, form, and sculpt the features onto your cake like the cheeks and chin. Depending on the kind of figure you're making, you may even want to add the nose at this point. This particular figure has a small enough nose that we will just be adding it later with buttercream.

*As a cake decorator you frequently wash your hands anyways- but definitely before and after this step you will really want to be thorough!

STEP 7

Chill the head in the fridge for 30 minutes. Pipe buttercream on the whole head and press it in with your off-set spatula. Smooth it over using the flexible cake scraper to give all your features definition. Chill the head in the freezer for 30 minutes so that it is firm enough to pick up with your hands.

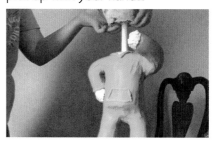

STEP 8

Use an off-set spatula under your wooden cake board to lift it up. Gently thread the hole in your cake board through the PVC pipe.

STEP 9

Replace the 45 degree elbow slip on your PVC pipe.

STEP 10

Cover it with more of your cake pop mixture to form the pony tail.

STEP 11

Pipe skin colored buttercream over the face and smooth with your flexible cake scraper.

STEP 12

Place your fingers in a bowl of warm water and use that to smooth the buttercream on the face even more. Take care not to get it dripping wet.

STEP 13

If isomalt eyes are too daunting for you (I purchased instructions from Simicakes.com), you can easily pipe on eyes with buttercream.

STEP 14

Pipe on buttercream around the eye and smooth it out with your flexible cake scraper.

STEP 15

Pipe on the features of the face and details of the body with buttercream and writing tips. For the skirt and hair we'll be using different tips.

STEP 16

For 3D eye lashes, place melted chocolate in a piping bag, cut a small hole in the tip, and then pipe short lines of chocolate on wax paper. Place the wax paper on something curved. I used a paper towel roll that I cut in half. Place them in the fridge for 5 minutes to harden. You can skip this step and just pipe on the eyelashes with buttercream if you want.

Place the eyelashes on your cake and then pipe a layer of buttercream behind them to help hold them in place.

STEP 17

Pipe on the hair using the 233 grass tip. You can sprinkle some Pinball Sweetapolita sprinkles in her hair for some bling.

STEP 18

Pipe three rows of ruffles around your cake for the tutu using your 124 tip. With the narrow end facing down, shake your wrist back and forth as you go to create these ruffles.

RAPUNZEL TOWER

Build a cake structure. Here are two options for you: For both options you will need at least an inch thick wooden cake board for a base, 1/2 inch PVC pipe, drill, PVC pipe cutter, and 7/8 inch spade bit, to make the holes.

Option one: (This is the one I used this time.)
You will also need a foam cake drum and hot glue gun. Drill a 7/8 inch hole in both the wooden cake board and foam board. Put hot glue in the wooden cake board and then place the PVC pipe in the hole. Once the glue is dried, place the foam cake drum over the top of that and through the PVC pipe. This foam cake board will keep the cake away from the glue, give added stability, and also be used later to hold a skewer for Rapunzel's hair (you wouldn't be able to stand the skewer into a wood board).

Option two: You
will also need a floor flange (like the ones we used in the "assemble a cake structure" tutorial), wood screws, and PVC pipe adapter. Use your wood screws to attach your floor flange to the middle of your wooden cake board. Thread the

PVC adapter into the floor flange and place the 1/2 inch PVC pipe in this. This structure will be the most stable of the two and easier to transport a cake, but you will not be able to do the final step of pressing the skewer into the cake board for Rapunzel's hair. You can pick an alternate way of doing her hair such as piping it directly against the tower instead of having it hang down.

Once you have a cake structure, you can begin assembling your cake.

Materials needed: 6 inch round cake, 5 inch round cake, six 4 inch round cakes (all of my cakes are approximately 1 & 1/2 inches tall), apple corer, off-set spatula, bench scraper, flexible cake scraper, serrated knife, buttercream, gel food coloring, 6 inch round cardboard cake circle, two 4 inch round cardboard cake circles, 8 smoothie straws, wood skewer, two sugar cones, piping tips 233, 5, 366, 47, 12, & 21, piping bags.

STEP 1

Cut a hole in the center of all your cardboard cake circles. Place the 6 inch round cake on the 6 inch round cardboard circle. Smooth a layer of buttercream and place the 5 inch round cake on that. Place all of these on a plate or larger cake circle so that it will be easier to transport to the fridge. Use your serrated knife to trim and round off the top edge, stopping to create a triangle in one spot for Rapunzel's window.

STEP 2

Use a pastry bag to cover these cakes in buttercream.

STEP 3

Scrape the bottom half of the cake with your bench scraper so that these edges will be straight.

STEP 4

The flexible cake scraper will be used on the top to give it the curved look. Place this cake in the fridge.

STEP 5

Stack your 4 inch cakes in two stacks that are each three cakes high. Use your apple corer to cut out the center of these cakes. Thread these cakes one at a time through your PVC pipe, applying a layer of buttercream between each layer. Stop when you get three cakes high to place your first layer of supports.

STEP 6

Place your first smoothie straw in your cakes, between the PVC pipe and the edge of your cake, taking care to keep it completely straight. Press it in until it touches your cake board. Use a toothpick and some gel food coloring to mark the smoothie straw where it is level with the top of the cakes. Use scissors to cut your smoothie straw and then mark and cut three more.

STEP 7

Place all of the cut smoothie straws into your three cakes, spacing them out evenly. Make sure that they are completely straight when going in because if you press them in at an angle, they will break the side of your cakes. These supports are very important because they will be supporting the entire load of your cake.

STEP 8

Cut a hole in your four inch card board cake circles. Place one of the cake circles on top of your first three cakes.

STEP 9

Repeat steps 5-8 to stack and support your next three cakes. You should now have buttercream between each layer, a second layer or straw support, and a cardboard cake circle on top of all of them.

STEP 10

Use a pastry bag to apply buttercream to your tower of cakes.

95

STEP 11

Press all the buttercream into your tower using your off-set spatula.

STEP 12

Smooth the tower with your flexible cake scraper.

STEP 13

Create some two-toned gray buttercream. In one bowl, use a tiny drop of black gel food coloring and mix well. In the second bowl, use double the amount of gel food coloring and mix well. Drop in a heaping tablespoon of the darker gray into the lighter gray buttercream's bowl. Fold over the dark gray buttercream into the light gray, but do not mix well. You want this to look marbled. Spoon this buttercream into your piping bag, prepared with the number 12 round piping tip.

STEP 14

Pipe stones onto the tower using the same method that we used to make scales in Waves and Scales. Starting at the bottom, pipe a dot, release the pressure on your bag and then press into your dot with your tip and drag your tip to the side. Pipe the next dot on the tail of the previous dot.

STEP 15

Retrieve your top cake from the fridge. Place your bench scraper under the cake board, supporting these cakes, and work it around the bottom until you can get your hands under it. Thread the cake board and cakes through the PVC pipe until it rests on your tower.

STEP 16

Check to make sure your PVC pipe is as tall as you want it. You should have a little bit sticking up to support the ice cream cone. Use your PVC pipe cutter to cut it. Pipe a layer of buttercream around the PVC pipe.

STEP 17

Place the sugar cone on top of your cake.

STEP 18

Use a wooden skewer to mark off everywhere that you will be piping details.

STEP 19

Pipe black buttercream in the window and smooth it off with your flexible cake scraper.

STEP 20

Using your number 47 piping tip (what we used for basket weaving), pipe wooden details in brown buttercream. Make sure that the serrated side is facing up.

STEP 21

With purple buttercream, smooth some on the sugar cone so that your roof tiles have somewhere to stick. Use the number 47 piping tip again with the purple buttercream to make your roof tiles. This time make sure that the smooth end of your tip is facing out and the serrated end is facing your cake. Pipe starting at the base of your roof and work your way up. To make each tile, pipe pulling down about half an inch. Pipe one row of tiles all around the base of your roof. Then pipe the next row above that one, overlapping the first row of tiles.

STEP 22

Smooth green buttercream on the bottom of your cake board with your off-set spatula. Add swirling vine details by using your number 5 round piping tip and green buttercream. After you're done with the vines you can add some leaves with the 366 tip. Pipe a leaf on your vine by piping out some green buttercream, let the leaf build, release the pressure on your piping bag, and then pull out.

STEP 23

Cut the tip off your second sugar cone and use a little bit of buttercream to attach it to your tower. Pipe some purple tiles on this one as well.

STEP 24

Using an extra long wooden skewer, cut it so that it reaches just to Rapunzel's window. Press this wooden skewer firmly into your foam cake board until you feel it go in. (You will not be able to do this if you're only using a wooden cake board.)

STEP 25

With your number 21 open star piping tip, in your pastry bag filled with gold buttercream, thread the pipe tip through the skewer, all the way down until it touches your board and the skewer is sticking out the end of your pastry bag (Your pastry bag will need to be open for this and not twisted on the end like it normally is.)

STEP 26

Applying pressure to your pastry bag to pipe the buttercream, pull it up slowly as you go until you reach the top.

STEP 27

Close up your piping bag and pipe the details of Rapunzel's hair coming from the window and piping it to attach to your wooden skewer.

STEP 28

For your final details pipe patches of grass using your 233 tip and green buttercream.

I absolutely love buttercream flowers! These are some of my favorite things to make when cake decorating. Many of these varieties- like the rose- are very common when cake decorating, but several you may have never seen before.

I love to get my inspiration from real flowers. By studying their intricacies and subtle color changes, I found I could create a more lifelike product. One of my favorite compliments is when people are afraid to eat them because they look so real!

Sometimes when hiking with my kids, I see beautiful flowers and start planning how I can make a buttercream version. How many people do that?? I've become a crazy cake lady, but I'm okay with that. Perhaps I can convert you too.

Buttercream Flowers

When piping flowers, you will need a very stiff buttercream. Follow my (mock) American Buttercream recipe, but add an additional 2 cups of confectioner's sugar to transform it into our decorating buttercream.

WHITE MINI FLOWER

Tools you'll need: Ateco 124 tip (note that the Ateco is thinner than the Wilton 124 tip) in a piping bag filled with white buttercream and a number 5 tip (round writing tip) in a piping bag filled with green buttercream. You can pipe a flower on a mini cupcake or on a parchment square on a flower nail. I'll show you how to pipe it on a mini cupcake.

STEP 1

Using your 124 tip with the narrow end facing out and the thicker end in the middle, apply pressure to your piping bag while turning your cupcake and pivot your wrist in the opposite direction.

STEP 2

Release pressure on your piping bag, and drag your tip down the cupcake to end the petal.

STEP 3

Tuck the next petal slightly under the petal you just finished and repeat the first two steps.

STEP 4

Continue piping petals until you fill your entire mini cupcake.

STEP 5

Pipe three dots in the center of your flower using the green buttercream and writing tip.

COLOR STRIPED MINI FLOWER

Tools you'll need: Wilton 104 (small petal tip). Prepare your piping bag using the color striping technique that you can see in the rose tutorial. Use a pink gel to stripe the bag and then fill it with a pink buttercream. You will also need a number 5 tip (round writing tip) in a piping bag filled with green buttercream. You can pipe the flower on a mini cupcake or on a parchment square on a flower nail. I'll show you how to pipe it on a mini cupcake.

STEP 1

Using your 104 tip, starting about half way on your cupcake, pipe a ring of petals. With the narrow, color-striped end facing out, pipe each petal using an up and down U motion.

STEP 2

Pipe an inner layer of petals over the outer ring of petals.

STEP 3

Pipe three dots in the middle of your flower using the green buttercream and writing tip.

BEGINNER'S, ADVANCED, GIANT & HIGHLIGHTED
ROSES

BEGINNER'S ROSES

When piping flowers, especially roses, you will need a stiffer buttercream for them to really hold their shape well. Using my (mock) American buttercream recipe, add an additional two cups of confectioner's sugar. I call these "beginner's roses" just to differentiate between the "advanced roses". The beginner's roses are piped with a Wilton 124 tip which is thicker than the Ateco 124 tip that I use for advanced roses. Really the main difference between the two is that the thicker tip is easier to control which is why I would use it if I was first learning how to pipe a rose. Once you build your confidence, try the Ateco 124 tip. This thinner tip makes thinner, more fragile and life-like looking petals. Also, because the petals are thinner, you're able to pipe quite a few more for a more realistic looking rose. Roses are actually the most advanced buttercream flower and take a bit of practice, but you can totally do it! I'll break it down to some simple of steps in this tutorial.

Tools you'll need for piping roses on a flower nail: stiff buttercream, gel food coloring, piping bag, Wilton 124 tip, wooden skewer, parchment squares, scissors, and a flower nail.

STEP 1

Check exactly where you want to cut your piping bag to insert your tip. You want your tip to sit snuggly halfway through your piping bag without popping out. (Always cut less rather than more because you can always cut more if you need to, but you don't want to cut it too large and ruin your piping bag.)

STEP 2

Slide your tip through your bag making sure that the narrow end lines up with a seam.

STEP 3

Fold your piping bag in half so that you don't get food coloring and buttercream on your hands when you fill it. It keeps things less messy and makes it easier to hold your bag when it's time to fill it.

STEP 4

On the seam that lines up with the narrow end, place a drop of gel food coloring. Use your wooden skewer to push the food coloring down the seam and all the way to the narrow end of your tip.

STEP 5

Your bag is now ready to fill with buttercream! The fuller it is, the harder it is to control and the harder you will have to press to pipe the buttercream. Use half as much buttercream if it's your first time piping a rose and then add more as you gain confidence.

STEP 6

Shake the buttercream down your bag and then press it down towards the tip. Give it a test squeeze to make sure both colors are coming out.

STEP 7

Dab a little bit of buttercream on your flower nail to act as glue for your parchment square.

STEP 8

How you hold your bag when piping is very important. You've already pressed your buttercream down towards the tip. Now you want to keep it tight so it does not come back up out the back of your piping bag. Give the bag a good twist here to keep the buttercream in it's place. Hold the twist in place with your thumb. You will be using your top couple of fingers to apply pressure to the buttercream which will squeeze it out the tip. As you pipe, you will want to squeeze down the buttercream and twist the bag in place again. The tighter you keep the bag the less work piping will be.

STEP 9

In a separate bag place some buttercream and cut a small hole in the tip. Piping straight down on the flower nail, pipe a small cone that you can use to start piping your petals on.

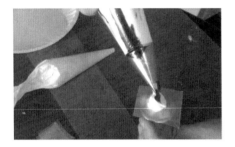

STEP 10

The first petal will need to pipe all around the cone. With the narrow color end up and tilted slightly in toward the center of the cone, apply a steady pressure on your piping bag as you slowly spin the flower nail.

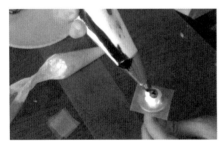

STEP 11

When the two ends of your first petal meet, release the pressure, and keep spinning your flower nail to end it.

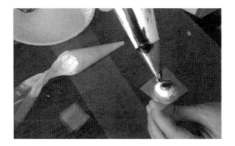

STEP 12

Now you can pipe the next three petals which will be cupping the cone and overlapping each other. Keeping the narrow end of your tip up, slightly turn your flower nail, while applying pressure to your piping bag, for each petal.

STEP 13

Pipe the next row of petals the same way but adding one or two more as the size of the center grows.

STEP 14

To open your rose, instead of pointing the narrow end of your tip towards the center of the rose, start pointing it outward toward yourself.

STEP 15

Your rose is done! Now you can slide it on a plate or container and place it in your freezer. When it hardens, you can easily pick up your rose and place it where you want it on your cake.

*The bonus of making roses on a parchment square is that you can make them a month or two in advance if needed. As long as you keep them in an airtight container, they will remain fresh tasting.

STEP 16

Grab a corner of the parchment square and gently drag it to the plate or container that you need to place it on.

IF YOU DON'T USE PARCHMENT SQUARES...

remove the rose from the flower nail directly and place it immediately on your cake using cake decorating scissors. You can use regular scissors. It's just slightly more difficult because regular scissors are not off-set, but it can still be done.

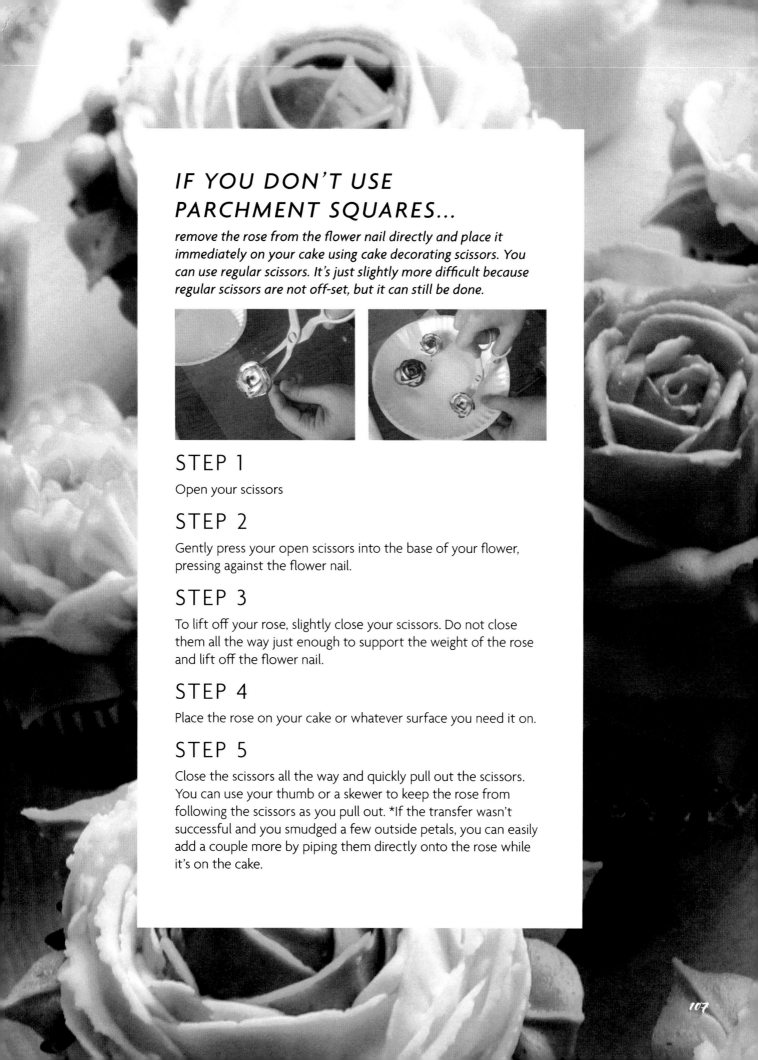

STEP 1

Open your scissors

STEP 2

Gently press your open scissors into the base of your flower, pressing against the flower nail.

STEP 3

To lift off your rose, slightly close your scissors. Do not close them all the way just enough to support the weight of the rose and lift off the flower nail.

STEP 4

Place the rose on your cake or whatever surface you need it on.

STEP 5

Close the scissors all the way and quickly pull out the scissors. You can use your thumb or a skewer to keep the rose from following the scissors as you pull out. *If the transfer wasn't successful and you smudged a few outside petals, you can easily add a couple more by piping them directly onto the rose while it's on the cake.

ADVANCED
ROSES

The advanced rose is created using the Ateco 124 tip. This thinner tip makes thinner more fragile and life-like looking petals. Also because the petals are thinner, you're able to pipe quite a few more for a more realistic looking rose.

Here's another way to color stripe your piping bag. Instead of using a strip of gel, you can use a more subtle color stripe by using two different colors of frosting. One color to stripe your bag and one color to fill your bag.

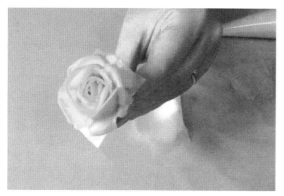

You can use a small off-set spatula or a knife to color stripe your bag with one of the buttercream colors. Just like you followed the seam of the bag to the narrow end of your tip with your gel food coloring, we're going to press the first color of buttercream in a line down the seam to the tip with our spatula. The bag is folded in half to help hold

it in place and because we're only going to fill it half way up with buttercream (or less if you need more control).

Fill it with the second color, press down your buttercream in the bag and twist to hold it in place. You can do a test squeeze to make sure both colors are coming through before piping your roses.

Follow the same steps for piping roses as you did for the beginner's rose, only we will be piping more petals because the thinner petals give us more room to make fuller roses. You will notice when piping that the tips of the petals tend to slightly curl outward giving the petals a more realistic look. This occurs naturally because of how thin the Ateco 124 tip is.

You can also pipe these roses on regular or mini cupcakes to make a beautiful cupcake garden!

GIANT ROSES

Are you ready? The Giant Rose is going to be as big as your open hand. You can use either 124 tip for this, but I'll show you using the Ateco 124 tip.

You're going to pipe this rose using a turntable to spin it as you would a flower nail. Turn a plate upside down on it and a large piece of parchment paper to cover it. To keep the plate from moving around on the turntable you can put a non-slip mat under it. Also to glue your parchment paper to the plate, use a little bit of buttercream.

Fill two piping bags as you normally would when piping roses. One with the tip of the bag cut off and the other with the 124 tip in.

STEP 1

First we're going to make a pad for our rose. This will help when piping our petals and later to safely and easily remove our rose. Pipe the pad as large as you want your actual rose to be.

STEP 2

Now we're going to build up a large cone in the middle for our center.

STEP 3

Follow the steps that we did in the beginner's rose to pipe this giant rose. Only we are going to continue piping more petals until we fill in the entire rose.

STEP 4

Pop the rose in the freezer for about 30 minutes. Now we can remove the rose to place it on our cake or wherever we need to place it using a knife. Slide a sharp knife under the rose and slide it all the way around the base, slowly peeling the parchment paper off.

STEP 5

With your fingers and knife under the rose, you can lift it and place it where you need it.

I placed mine on a little plate just for demonstration and then added gold highlights. Check out the next page for how to add gold highlights!

GOLD
HIGHLIGHTS

You will need: 100% gold luster dust (like this Sterling Pearl from *The Sugar Art*), a food-safe paint brush, and an alcohol based liquid like Vodka or Clear Vanilla extract.

The alcohol will evaporate as the paint dries. I usually use clear vanilla extract because that's what I have on hand.

Start with about a fourth a teaspoon of the gold dust in a small bowl. Add the liquid just a tiny bit at a time. You really only want enough liquid to make this into a paint.

Whatever buttercream rose you're painting, make sure it's been in the freezer for about 30 minutes so that

the buttercream is stiff and doesn't come off on your paint brush when you paint. Start in the middle of your rose and work your way out, painting the edges of all your petals.

PEONY

Tools you'll need: Wilton 124 tip, Russian piping tip, two colors of buttercream. You can pipe the Peony on a cupcake or on a large parchment square on your turntable.

STEP 1

Here's the Russian piping tip I used for the middle. Fill the piping bag with yellow buttercream.

STEP 2

Smooth a thin layer of buttercream on your cupcake or parchment square so that the piping buttercream has something to stick to. Pipe once with the Russian piping tip directly down in the center of the cupcake.

STEP 3

Using the Wilton 124 tip, with your narrow end up, pipe four petals cupping the yellow center.

STEP 4

Continue piping petals around the center, only with these petals, each time you pipe, shake your wrist while piping to create a ruffly look. When ending a petal, release the pressure on your bag and push the tip in toward the flower.

STEP 5

Like a rose, slowly open your Peony petals by tipping the narrow end of the tip slightly more outward each time.

STEP 6

When you're at the last row of petals, the tip will be flat as you pipe, making sure the narrow end is on the outside.

PANSY

Tools you'll need: two 124 tips, and purple, white, and yellow buttercream. You can pipe the Pansy directly onto a cupcake. You can also pipe it on a piece of wax paper on your turntable and then freeze it to place on a cake later. The Pansy consists of five overlapping petals, two solid, and three multi colored.

STEP 1

Prepare your piping bag by filling one with a solid purple buttercream. The second bag will use the multi-color method. Placing a piece of plastic wrap on the counter, pipe a thick line of purple, a thin line of white on that (to act as a buffer between the purple and yellow so it doesn't muddy the colors), and then a thick line of yellow.

STEP 2

Roll it like a burrito, twisting one end, and cutting the end off the other. Place that one in your other piping bag.

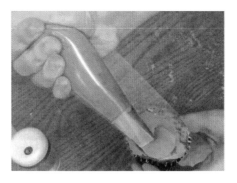

STEP 3

After placing a thin coat of buttercream on your cupcake, pipe the first petal. Starting at the middle of your cupcake, with the narrow end out (the narrow end will always be the edge for each petal), pipe straight out and pivot your tip around while continuing pressure on your piping bag. Continue through the 180 pivot, pulling the tip in toward the center of the cupcake, releasing the pressure on your bag while pulling to end the petal.

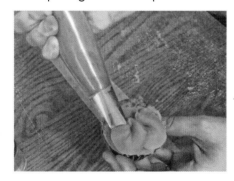

STEP 4

Begin in the middle again and pipe another solid petal, overlapping the last one.

STEP 5

Using the multi-colored tip, pipe two petals overlapping the solid ones, directly across from each other.

STEP 6

The final petal will overlap the two multicolored ones. This one will be piped right in the middle and over the top of them.

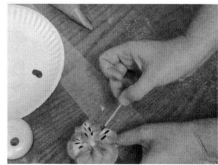

STEP 7

The final touch will be to dip a toothpick in some purple gel food coloring and gently add the dark purple lines over the multicolored petals.

SUNFLOWER

What you'll need: Wilton tip 233 (grass tip), Wilton tip 366 (leaf tip)

STEP 1

Smooth your cupcake with buttercream to give your petals something to stick to. Pipe your first row of petals about a finger tip in from the outer edge of your cupcake. Pipe a petal with yellow buttercream using the 366 tip, let it build, releasing the pressure on your piping bag while pulling the petal out.

STEP 2

Pipe an entire row of petals for the outside circle of petals.

STEP 3

Pipe a second row of petals in front of the outer circle, overlapping the petals.

STEP 4

Using the 233 tip with brown or chocolate buttercream, pipe once directly in the center of your cupcake. Pipe straight down. Release the pressure on your piping bag as you pull up.

STEP 5

Pipe a row circling the center dot and overlapping a small portion of the yellow petals.

CARNATION

Tools you'll need: Ateco 124 tip (note that the Ateco is thinner than the Wilton 124 tip), two colors of buttercream. You can pipe the carnation on a mini or regular cupcake or on a large parchment square on your turntable. I'll show you how to pipe it on a mini cupcake. It's the exact same way that you will pipe it on a larger cupcake, only for the larger one, you would continue piping petals until you filled the cupcake.

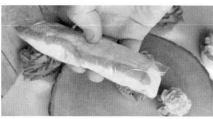

STEP 1

We will use the multiple color approach when preparing the piping bag. In the plastic wrap pipe one thin line of buttercream and then add the main color. Wrap the plastic in a burrito, twisting one end and cutting open the end that will go down into your piping bag prepared with your Ateco 124 tip. *For a more defining color line, pipe a thicker line in your plastic wrap before adding the main color.

STEP 2

In a separate piping bag filled with the secondary color, cut off a small portion of the tip and pipe a cone in the center of your cupcake.

STEP 3

Using the Ateco 124 tip, narrow end facing up, you're going to pipe a ruffle straight out. Touch your tip to the cone and shake your hand back and forth, slowing pulling straight out. (We're not wrapping a petal around the cone at this time)

STEP 4

After doing the first ruffle straight out, continue piping straight out ruffles around the cone.

STEP 5

The cone will be completely surrounded in ruffles that are piped straight out from the cone.

STEP 6

Now it's time to start wrapping the cone with ruffly petals. Using the same back and forth shaking motion, wrap ruffly short petals around the center.

STEP 7

Continue wrapping around the center with short ruffly petals until the carnation is full. The outer petals will be more open. Tilt the narrow end of the tip slightly outward to open the petals. *If you're piping a carnation on a regular sized cupcake instead of a mini, continue piping petals until the cupcake is full. The last row of petals will be made with the tip almost completely flat with the narrow end pointed out toward the edge of the cupcake.*

STEP 8

Optional: add some green leaves using green buttercream and the 352 leaf tip.

RUSSIAN PIPING TIP FLOWERS

Russian Piping tips are a great way to easily add beautiful flowers to your cake. I used a variety of the flower tips. Some look like roses and some have little holes in the center surrounded by petals, but you use them all the same. You will need to make sure you're using the stiff decorating buttercream when piping with the Russian piping tips otherwise you will just be piping blobs instead of flowers with defined petals. You will also need to make sure that you've crumb coated your cake before you start so that the flowers have something to stick to. I used Americolor gel food coloring to color the buttercream. I picked four different tips and colors for these flowers.

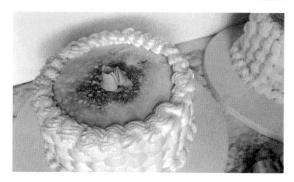

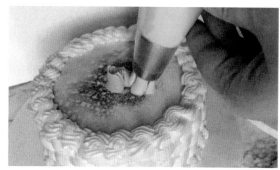

STEP 1

Starting in the center of the cake, you will pipe your first flower.

STEP 2

Press your top straight down into the cake. Apply pressure to your piping bag. Squeeze and let a small mound of buttercream build. As you pull up, continue the pressure on your piping bag so that the petals grow a little longer.

STEP 3

Release the pressure on your piping bag but continue to pull up.

STEP 4

Continue piping flowers all around the center flower, working your way out and alternating the colored flowers.

STEP 5

Using a 352 or similar leaf tip, pipe leaves in between the flowers to fill in the rest of your foliage.

Holiday Cupcakes

In my school of thought, there must be a cupcake for every occasion. If you're carving a turkey for the big holiday meal, you should probably have a smaller, more ridiculous turkey to carve for dessert.

I realize plum pudding or pumpkin pie is more traditional for the holiday season, but let's be serious-I'd prefer a cupcake shaped like a Christmas tree to a fruitcake any day.

Peruse this section for some ideas for alternative desserts that might just become new family favorites.

PUMPKIN
DECORATED CUPCAKES

Tools you'll need: A size 5 & 7 writing tip and a 1M large star tip, and orange, brown, and green buttercream.

STEP 1

Starting at the center of the cupcake with the 1M tip and orange buttercream, pipe a swirl of buttercream.

STEP 2

Continue piping around, making a smaller swirl on top of the last one.

STEP 3

Using the number 7 tip and brown buttercream, pipe a stem straight on top of your pumpkin.

STEP 4

With the green buttercream and size 5 tip, start at the stem and pipe a green spiral down the side of your pumpkin.

TURKEY
DECORATED CUPCAKES

*I can't get over how cute these little guys turned out!
Fortunately for everyone, they don't taste like poultry.*

*What you'll need: A 352 leaf tip, and 5, 7, & 12 writing
tips (if you don't have a variety of writing tip sizes, you
can also just cut different size holes in your piping bags
for the different sizes) and red, orange, yellow, brown,
white, and black buttercream.*

STEP 1

With the red buttercream and 352 leaf tip, pipe an almost full circle of red feathers around the outer circle of the cupcake.

STEP 2

Pipe a second row of red feathers half overlapping the first one.

STEP 3

Pipe a row of orange feathers half over lapping the last row of feathers.

STEP 4

Next pipe a row of yellow feathers, and then fill the remaining portion of the cupcake with yellow feathers.

STEP 5

With the large, size 12 writing tip and brown buttercream, pipe the body of the turkey. Pipe a line straight up about halfway up the cupcake and then back down a short ways for the head.

STEP 6

Pipe the beak with orange buttercream using the number 5 tip.

STEP 7

With the number 7 and white buttercream, pipe on the whites of his eyes. With the number 5 tip and black buttercream, pipe the center of his eyes.

STEP 8

With red buttercream and the number 5 tip, pipe from one side of the top of the turkey's beak, across and then pulling down a little bit on the other side.

SNOWFLAKE
DECORATED CUPCAKES

STEP 1

Melt the candy melts in the microwave at 30 second intervals, mixing them between each interval until they are smooth.

STEP 2

I printed out a sheet of paper with a bunch of snowflakes on it and placed it under my wax paper to act as a guide. You can also free hand your own design if you don't find something online that you want to print out. Tape down your wax paper to a piece of card board to keep it from moving.

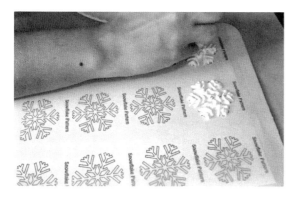

STEP 3

Pour the melted candy melts into a piping bag that's prepared with a size 5 tip. Keep the tip up until you're ready to pipe your first snowflake because gravity will push the candy melt out before you're ready if your tip is pointing down. Pipe snowflakes on a piece of wax paper with the melts.

STEP 4

Pipe only a few snowflakes at a time and then sprinkle them with silver Diamondust and place a small silver sugar pearl in the center. The reason I only do a few at a time is so that the sprinkles will stick. Let them sit until firm. If you need to speed up the process, place them in the fridge. If you are putting them in the fridge, make sure that your wax paper is on something you can pick up and move like a cake board.

STEP 5

Use a 1M tip and pale blue buttercream to pipe swirls on your cupcakes. I used a drop Americolor Sky Blue gel food coloring. I only pipe 3 cupcakes at a time and then sprinkle them with regular sized white sugar pearls and tiny pearls. The sprinkles will not stick if you wait too long to sprinkle them which is why I only do three at a time.

STEP 6

Place a snowflake in the center of each of the three cupcakes that you completed so that they stick as well.

  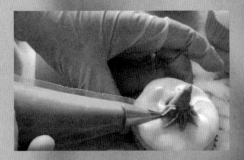

STEP 1

Cut the tip off of your sugar cone using a serrated knife.

STEP 2

Using a large round piping tip, pipe white buttercream starting in the center and then piping around until the cupcake is cover in white buttercream.

STEP 3

Press down on the tip of the sugar cone in the middle of the cupcake. Pipe green buttercream on the cone using the small star tip. Starting at the bottom of the cone, press the tip on the cone and apply pressure to your bag. Pull the tip toward you while still applying pressure. Release the pressure and continue pulling out. Pipe all the way around the bottom and then add another layer around until you work your way to the top of the cone.

Tools you'll need: Large round piping tip, small round piping tips, small star tip (like a #13), tiny sprinkles, sugar cones, serrated knife, crusting buttercream (like my mock buttercream recipe) colors: white, green, red, orange, yellow, and black.

SNOWMAN SCENE
DECORATED CUPCAKES

STEP 4

Sprinkle the tree with your choice of sprinkles before the buttercream crusts. I always sprinkle the tree right after piping or else the buttercream won't be sticky enough to stick to.

STEP 5

Pipe a dot of yellow buttercream at the top of your tree for the star, using a small round piping tip.

STEP 6

With the large round piping tip and white buttercream, pipe a large round ball. Pipe the round ball by applying pressure to your piping bag and letting the ball build until it is nice and round for the base of our snowman.

STEP 7

Give the snowman base a couple of minutes to crust before piping the next ball on top for the second part of the snowman. I usually pipe all of my snowmen bases on all the cupcakes first, and then I come back to the one I started on first as it will be ready for the next ball. Using the same tip, pipe the next ball on top of the first ball.

STEP 8

Use red buttercream and a small round tip to make the scarf. Pipe around the snowman's neck and then make a little tail for the scarf to hang down in front.

STEP 9

Using black buttercream and a small round tip, pipe the eyes. Pipe the hat on top by letting it build, pulling up while continuing the pressure and then releasing the pressure, continue pulling up. After a couple minutes the buttercream will crust and you can gently tap down the point on the top of the hat so that it is more flat.

If you want to turn these into Snow Globe Cupcakes, continue on to the next tutorial...

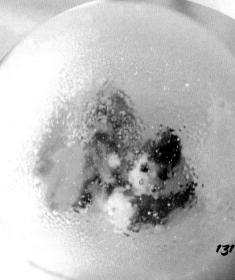

STEP 10

Pipe the orange buttercream with a small round piping tip. Keep up the pressure on your bag as you pull out and to the side, release the pressure and keep pulling out.

SNOW GLOBE
DECORATED CUPCAKES

Tools you'll need: Isomalt, silicone spheres, silicone mat

Isomalt is a sugar substitute, store away in a cool dry place, away from moisture and not in the fridge. I place my domes on my cupcakes right before serving because if they're in contact with the buttercream for too long, they start to look more cloudy.

You will want pre-cooked isomalt if you don't want to cook your own. I buy my pre-cooked isomalt from Simicakes. All you have to do is microwave it and it's great quality.

Caution: Isomalt is super hot when it's heated and will cause burns if you get it on your skin.

Silicone spheres: they need to be a food-safe, heat-safe, silicone. I bought mine on Amazon. Each sphere was a little over two inches wide.

STEP 1

Place your pre-cooked isomalt tiles or pieces into a microwave-safe dish. I used a silicone dish because you can just peel out the leftover isomalt and reuse it later. Heat it at 30 second intervals, stirring each time.

STEP 2

Once it is boiling, wait for the boiling to stop and then pour it into one of the silicone spheres, filling it about halfway up.

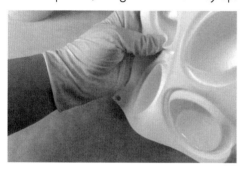

STEP 3

Cautiously tilt your sphere around, making sure the isomalt touches all the sides of the sphere and to the top without going over the edge. Definitely don't get the isomalt on your hands. Let the isomalt travel around a second time, coating the whole sphere completely twice.

STEP 4

Tip the sphere upside down over your dish that you used to heat the isomalt in. Let it drip down for a few minutes.

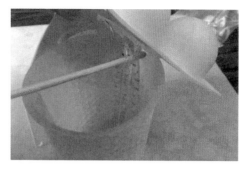

STEP 5

Use a wooden skewer or spoon to grab the tails of isomalt that are dripping down and gently twist and pull them off.

STEP 6

You can now tip your sphere over onto your silicone mat to completely cool. I used a portable fan to speed up the process. Do not place in the fridge.

STEP 7

Once the isomalt is completely cool to the touch, gently pull the top and sides back and slowly peel it out. Isomalt is very breakable and can easily shatter so you'll want to do this part slowly.

CHRISTMAS TREE
DECORATED CUPCAKES

Tools you'll need: A size 7 writing tip, 4B large French tip, and red and green buttercream and sprinkles

STEP 1

Starting at the center of the cupcake with the 4B tip and green buttercream, pipe a swirl of buttercream. Continue piping around, making a smaller swirl on top of the last one. Make sure you leave enough room at the outer edge of your cupcake for the tree skirt.

STEP 2

Optional: Using the number 7 tip and red buttercream, pipe a tree skirt all around the outer edge of the cupcake.

STEP 3

Sprinkle your tree with ornaments. You can also top your tree with a gold sugar pearl or you can choose to use yellow buttercream and a small star tip for the star on top.

SANTA HAT

DECORATED CUPCAKES

Tools you'll need: A size 2A writing tip, 21 star tip, red, and white buttercream

STEP 1

Pipe a swirl of red buttercream using the 12 writing tip.

STEP 2

Pipe a border around the hat with the white buttercream and 21 star tip. Lastly pipe one star right on top.

WREATH

DECORATED CUPCAKES

Tools you'll need: A size 5 writing tip, 21 star tip, red, green, and white buttercream

STEP 1

Smooth white buttercream over your cupcake. Next pipe a circle of stars around the outside of your cupcake with the 21 star tip and green buttercream. Pipe straight down for each star.

STEP 2

Using the 5 writing tip and red buttercream draw a red bow at the top and pipe little red dots for the berries.

POINSETTIA
DECORATED CUPCAKES

Tools you'll need: Tips 366, 5, & 2A, buttercream (green, white, and red), Wilton's gold sugar pearls.

STEP 1

Pipe a circle of green buttercream around the edge of your cupcakes using the 2A tip.

STEP 2

Use the 366 tip to pipe the outer layer of petals. Start close to the center, apply pressure to your piping bag and lightly shake your wrist as you pull out, release the pressure on your bag, and continue pulling out. Let each petal slightly over lap as you fill in the entire outer circle of petals.

STEP 3

Pipe the inner layer of petals, starting in the middle, and overlapping the outer petals.

STEP 4

Using the number 5 tip, pipe a dot of green buttercream in the center of your cupcake. Circle this dot with green dots.

STEP 5

Using Wilton's gold sugar pearls, place these on the green dots.

REINDEER
DECORATED CUPCAKES

No reindeer were harmed in the making of these cupcakes.

Note: This photo is made with mini cupcakes, but the tutorial is with regular sized ones. You can make them the exact same way! Just less icing for the tiny ones.

Tools you'll need: Mini chocolate chips, a size 2A, 7, & 5 writing tip, and chocolate, white, red, and black buttercream.

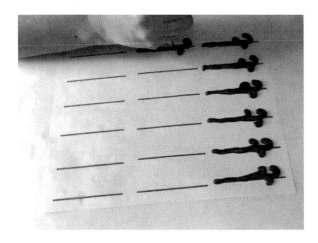

STEP 1

Melt the mini chocolate chips in the microwave at 30 second intervals, mixing the chocolate chips between each interval until they are smooth.

STEP 2

Pour the melted chocolate into a piping bag that's prepared with a size 5 tip. Keep the tip up until you're ready to pipe your first antler because gravity will push the chocolate out before you're ready if your tip is pointing down. Pipe antlers on a piece of wax paper with the chocolate. To make sure that my antlers are straight, I print out a page of straight lines and put that under my wax paper. As you pipe your straight lines with chocolate, make a little hook on either side of the line in staggered locations near the top half of the antler.

After piping your chocolate antlers, let them sit until firm. If you need to speed up the process, place them in the fridge. You will need to make sure that your wax paper is on something you can pick up and move like a cake board in order to move it into the fridge.

STEP 4

Peel your chocolate antlers off the wax paper once they're hard. Gently push them into the center of your buttercream swirl.

STEP 5

With your number 7 tip, pipe on the eyes and then use the tip to pipe on the red nose. Use the number 5 tip to pipe on the center of the eyes.

*Note: If you prefer, you can swap the black and white on the eyes.

STEP 3

Pipe a swirl of chocolate buttercream using the 2A writing tip.

QR Codes

Never heard of QR codes? No problem! These blocky black and white squares are actually barcodes that take you to a predetermined website; they are designed to be scanned with your smartphone. In many cases, your phone will come with a scanning app preloaded. With the app open, your phone will look like it's ready to take a photo, with a marked spot in the center.

That's where it wants you to put the QR code. Once it registers, the code will take your phone to the website correlated with the code.

In this case, most of these QR codes will take you to my YouTube tutorials! If you also like watching someone demonstrate techniques in a video, this spread is for you.

I'm making new tutorials and recipes all the time! I

had to stop myself from perpetually adding new ones to this book, or else I'd never be finished. The good news is, my YouTube channel is up to date. Please feel free to subscribe to my channel, *Icing on Top-Becky's Cakes*, and make sure your notifications are turned on for the latest content.

My Facebook Page

My Instagram Feed

My YouTube Channel

RECIPES

BASICS

(Mock) American Buttercream

Berry Filling

Basic Release, Level, Frost

Buttercream Marbling

Blackberry Buttercream

Candied Lemons

Filling a Cupcake

Marble Candy Melt Sail

Candied Strawberries

Caramel Buttercream & Filling

Pipe a Buttercream Scarf

Pipe Multiple Colors

Cherry Buttercream

Lemon Buttercream

Piping Basketweave on a Cake

Practice Piping Sheet

Mama's Fudge Filling

Mango Buttercream

Quick & Easy Fancy Cupcakes

Rice Paper Sails

Peanut Butter Buttercream

Peanut Butter Filling

Rosette Cake

Sprinkle Surprise

Pumpkin Buttercream

Strawberry Buttercream

Stack and Fill a Seminaked Cake

Waves & Scales

ADVANCED   FLOWERS

3D Ice Cream Cone

Anti Gravity Cake

Advanced Rose

Beginner's Rose

Assemble a Cake Structure

Buttercream Paneling

Carnation

Mini Flowers

Butterfly Bling

Chocolate Bowl

Pansy

Peony

Drip Cake

Flower Pot

Russian Piping Flower

Sunflower

Rapunzel

Standing Cake Figure

Stripes Cake

HOLIDAY

Christmas Tree

Poinsettia

Pumpkin

Reindeer

Santa Hat

Snowflake

Snow Globe

Snowman

Turkey

Index

Additional Credits

BECKY BEVERLY

Author, Photographer (all photographs unless otherwise noted)

ABIGAIL WALKER

Graphic Designer, Photographer (p. 4-5, 6-7)

RUTH ANN SCHWALBE

Copy Editor